D1158149

PRINCIPLES OF THE PHILOSOPHY OF THE FUTURE

The Library of Liberal Arts

PRINCIPLES OF THE PHILOSOPHY OF THE FUTURE

LUDWIG FEUERBACH

Translated, with an Introduction, by

MANFRED H. VOGEL

Assistant Professor of Religion, Northwestern University

The Library of Liberal Arts
published by
THE BOBBS-MERRILL COMPANY, INC.
A Subsidiary of Howard W. Sams & Co., Inc.
Publishers • Indianapolis • New York • Kansas City

Ludwig Feuerbach: 1804–1872

Grundsätze der Philosophie der Zukunft was first published in 1843.

Printed in the United States of America
Library of Congress Catalog Card Number: 64-66068
First Printing

Contents

Introduction

The awareness that Feuerbach has something significant to say and that he represents an important juncture in nineteenth-century cultural development has grown in recent years. As Sidney Hook rightly asserted as early as 1936:

The significance of the life and thought of Ludwig Feuerbach is only now emerging in contemporary philosophy. The rise of Marxism, the development of what is called *Existenzialphilosophie* in Germany (Heidegger, Jaspers), the renaissance of Hegelianism, and the increasing interest in the philosophy and psychology of religion have gradually brought Feuerbach into the field of vision of philosophic consciousness.[1]

Even more than the philosophers, the theologians of recent days have taken account of Feuerbach. Buber, Tillich, and Barth are just a few prominent examples.

No one among the modern philosophers has been so intensively, so exclusively and precisely occupied with the problem of theology as Feuerbach. . . . No philosopher of his time penetrated the contemporary theological situation as effectually as he, and few spoke with such pertinence. I would say further: the attitude of the antitheologian Feuerbach was more theological than that of many theologians.[2]

Feuerbach is coming to occupy an important position in the history of recent philosophies of man and culture. Any philosopher who has not completely succumbed to the notion of a scientific, technical philosophy and who is willing to reflect on the broader questions of "Who is man?" and "What is culture, civilization, society?" will find in Feuerbach's reflections an incentive and a challenge. Only to the extent that

[1] Sidney Hook, *From Hegel to Marx* (New York: Humanities Press, 1950), p. 220.

[2] Karl Barth, *Die Theologie und die Kirche* (Munich: Evangelische Verlag, 1928), II, 212.

modern philosophers have retreated from the traditional philosophical task of reflecting on the broad and basic questions of human existence—leaving a vacuum to be filled and monopolized almost exclusively by theologians—has the study of Feuerbach been surrendered by the faculties of philosophy to the theological seminaries. By right, he belongs to both, for both are concerned, though in different ways, with the problem of man.

Feuerbach is the philosopher of man. He is the philosophical anthropologist *par excellence*. It is in this broader sense of the word "religious," that is, the concern with human destiny, that he could assert that the whole of his philosophy was religion. And it is from the same viewpoint that he launches his intensive and persistent critique of what he regards as the aberration of religion, that is, of theology, of religion in the narrower sense.

This concern with human destiny is not something distinctive of Feuerbach. As a philosophical anthropologist, Feuerbach belongs to and is an authentic product of post-Kantian and, even more specifically, of post-Hegelian German philosophy. He can be understood only in this context. Hegel—be he interpreted as the great culminator or as the great initiator—is a focal point in German philosophy. None of his successors could escape his impact. He is the center around which philosophy in the first half of nineteenth-century Germany rotated. Feuerbach, far from being an exception, is directly and decisively related to Hegel. Although to say that "Feuerbach was Hegel's fate. . . . Feuerbach belongs to Hegel as much as the beaker of hemlock to Socrates" [3] may imply an interpretation of Hegel to which many scholars may take exception, certainly all can agree that Hegel was Feuerbach's necessary precondition. Feuerbach evolved his philosophical thinking against the constant background of Hegel's thought, first as a faithful disciple and subsequently as the archrebel. Throughout Feuerbach's creative and fruitful period of philosophical

[3] Hermann Glockner, *Die Voraussetzungen der Hegelschen Philosophie*, quoted in Hook, *From Hegel to Marx*, p. 220.

reflection, Hegel's philosophy exerted a determining influence on him, be it in a positive or a negative way. One can understand Feuerbach, like other post-Hegelian German philosophers, only in relation to Hegel.

My approach to Feuerbach in this essay will, therefore, involve the examination of these two central issues of his philosophy—his critique of religion (Section II) and his relation to Hegel (Section IV). These are, indeed, also the two central issues of his *Grundsätze der Philosophie der Zukunft,* which is offered here in translation. In this way, the *Principles* is, as indeed Feuerbach claimed, the culmination and summation of his philosophy. In order to set these two issues in a wider perspective, I shall also undertake in this Introduction to examine briefly the basic structure of Feuerbach's mature and distinct philosophic position (Section I), to trace his development from his earlier Hegelian position (Section III), and to place him in the context of post-Hegelian philosophy (Section V). Finally, I shall offer a short introduction to the work itself in order to trace its thematic structure (Section VI).

I

Feuerbach is one of those philosophers who in the course of their philosophic careers radically changed their views. He starts his work as a strict, down-the-line Hegelian idealist. Yet his philosophy in its positive and final presentation is thoroughly empirical. Feuerbach's distinct contribution is made as an empiricist, not as an idealist, and it is as such that we must analyze the structure and unity of his thought.

In its final and distinct formulation, Feuerbach's philosophy is based on sense perception as the primary source of cognition. Feuerbach turns to sense perception because of his conviction that true reality resides in the concrete, particular, individual being. He consistently and vehemently attacks the view that makes the universal the focus of reality. The universal is only a concept, a word, but not reality. One should not confuse the two, for "where words cease, life first begins,

and the secret of being is first disclosed."[1] Reality lies in the particular object, not in the concept or the universal. Making the universal represent reality would be to try to overcome "the contradiction between the word, which is general, and the object, which is always a particular" (§ 28). But this cannot be done. One cannot bridge the particular, which belongs to existence, with the general, which belongs to thought. There is "an immense difference . . . between the 'this' as an object of abstract thought and the 'this' as an object of reality" (§ 28). The 'this' as an object of reality must be objectively and concretely determined by space and time. Space and time are not mere forms of appearance, as they are for abstract thought. They are conditions of being. To-be-here is the primary act and certainty of being. "Here am I, and you are there" (§ 44). Thus, it is in the concrete, particular being which is spatially differentiated that we can encounter the truly real. The particularity of concrete being becomes the criterion for philosophy. Philosophy must be able to express and represent this particularity without distorting or transforming it into something else.

Philosophy can do this only if its prime organon of cognition is sense perception. Only sense perception, and not pure thought, is the means by which we can grasp concrete reality and thus true reality. "The real in its reality is . . . an object of the senses; it is the sensuous" (§ 32). For only specific determinations, and not the general logical-metaphysical determinations, give us true knowledge of the object, and they are perceived by the senses and not by abstract, pure thought (§ 49). It is a fundamental mistake to suppose that pure thought with its universals can incorporate and comprehend reality.

> A being that only thinks, and thinks abstractly, has no conception at all of being, of existence, or of reality. Being is the boundary of thought. . . . (§ 26)

Such thought which "overleaps its opposite," which "claims for itself what belongs not to itself but to being" (§ 29), is fundamentally wrong. The "this" as an object of reality, that

[1] Feuerbach, *Principles*, § 28 below.

is, a particular, individual object, can be grasped only by sense perception.

The emotions in general and, more particularly, the emotion of love, fit nicely into a philosophy based on sense perception. They occupy a valid and important position, for the emotions, too, refer to the concrete, particular individual. One does not love in general. One loves a concrete, particular object, not a universal. Thus, true reality is grasped not only in sense perception but also in the emotions. "Only in feeling and in love does . . . the particular 'this' have absolute value. . . . The secret of being discloses itself only in love," which is passion (§ 33). Not through cold, abstract thought, but only through involved passions is reality made known to man.

This is not to say, however, that Feuerbach's philosophy is irrational or that it advocates an obscurantism based merely on vague and undisciplined feeling and sensation. Feuerbach repeats again and again that this is not the case. The very function of a philosophy is to think and to formulate judgments in intellectual terms. Thought must, therefore, be an integral part of his philosophy. He freely admits that the world stands open only to the mind. But he wants man to admit that it must be an open mind and that the openings of the mind are the senses (§ 51). It is thought that is in harmony with the senses and does not wish to reject them (§ 36), that thinks in accordance with the appearance of things in reality and does not claim exemption from the laws that govern reality (§ 45), that does not lead away from but rather toward the sensuous object (§ 43). It is real and objective thought, determined and rectified by sensuous perception; it is not thought isolated for itself and in itself (§ 48). It is thought that takes matters in a broad sense, that does not autocratically limit the freedom and independence of the object, and that, while enlightening the mind, does not presume to decide or determine matters for it (§ 48). Such thought, that is, thought that is determined by sense perception, is accorded full honor and is accepted with open arms by Feuerbach.

What Feuerbach must reject, because for him reality resides

in the concrete, particular object, is that thought that claims to encompass in itself—and indeed itself be—the whole of reality. He must reject the abstract, pure thought of the idealistic, monistic world view that is based on the principle of the identity of thought and being. Such identity, he argues, is impossible; although it gives the appearance of identifying two distinct entities, in truth it is only a sham identity, of thought with itself. Thought is made the sum total of truth and reality. Only that that can be thought is true and real. In this way, being is made a predicate of reason and thought, and is incorporated into thought. What we have here, therefore, is no longer being as a separate and distinct entity, but the idea and thought of being. Thus, although the principle of identity presumes to identify being with thought, it is not truly being that is so identified, but only ideated being.

A being that is not distinguished from thought and that is only a predicate or a determination of reason is only an ideated and abstracted being; but in truth it is not being. The identity of thought and being expresses, therefore, only the identity of thought with itself. . . . (§ 24)

Only in pure thought can the appearance of the identity of being and thought be given. In truth, however, both the beginning and the end are in thought. Both the difference and the identity are posited within thought.

Thought places being in opposition to itself, but within itself, and thus it invalidates directly and without difficulty the opposition of being vis-à-vis itself; for being, as the opposition of thought within thought, is nothing other than an idea itself. (§ 24)

Thus, a monistic world view can be established in a philosophy that takes pure thought as its organon of cognition. It is a monistic view of reality as thought.

A philosophy based on sense perception must, however, reject this. For it, being must be determinate being that is independent of and precedes thought. It cannot be reduced to thought. Indeed, if sense perception discloses reality as it truly is, then there can be no ideated being. There can be no identity, nor can there be a monistic world view. Sense perception leads to a dualistic world view in which the subject is confronted by an irreducible object. No synthesis mediating the chasm between subject and object and thus attaining a higher identity of the two is possible (§ 24). Sense perception tears asunder the identity of thought with itself symbolized by the circle. It presents a polarity of subject-object, of nature and man, which is symbolized by the ellipse.

In this polarity, the object has its own irreducible reality, which cannot be mediated in a higher or more ultimate reality. It is not a moment that is only transitory in the process of thought. The object is ultimate and independent, facing the ego. The subject does not determine it; it determines itself. "The determinations that afford real knowledge are always only those that determine the object by the object itself, namely, by its own individual determinations" (§ 49). Sense perception honors and guards the independent reality of the object. It does not impose its own laws on the object. On the contrary, it conforms to it.

> Perception takes matters in a broad sense, whereas thought takes them in a narrow sense. Perception leaves matters in their unlimited freedom, whereas thought gives them laws, which, however, are only too often despotic. Perception enlightens the mind, but determines and decides nothing. . . . (§ 48)

Decision and determination are not in the hands of the subject whose means of cognition is sense perception. They are with the object.

Not only is the object no longer dependent on the subject; the object is now the determining factor. It is the object that determines the data given in sense perception, and consequently the subject must recognize reality in the object. There is no "subject" standing behind the object, thus making the object the property and the creation of the ego. Only by guarding the independence of the object and exposing itself to the object does the subject receive the "truth of reality."

This means that the subject, that is, the ego, is the recipient, the passive agent. For Feuerbach, man is indeed essentially passive and determined by the environment that surrounds him (§ 32). The essential attribute of man is "suffering," in the sense of being the recipient of the action of something else. This is the permanent state of man's being. Under no circumstances can it be changed.[2] Accordingly, Feuerbach's projected portrayal of man's realization and fulfillment does not change this basic relationship between man and nature. Realized man remains passive, "suffering," and determined by nature. Realization is not conceived in terms of man's concrete mastery over his destiny and nature or in terms of his mastery in thought. Fulfillment and realization are conceived, rather, in terms of "liberation" and the substitution of one kind of determination for another. Realization is constituted by man's liberation from the negative, oppressive, and unjustified determination of nature and by the removal of those needs and wants that are accidental and contingent, such as hunger and poverty. It means the liberation of man's passivity from those needs and wants that are painful and degrading. It means changing natural determination from "a source of privation and pain to one of abundance and fulfillment."[3] But man's passivity and "suffering" remain. Realized man is still determined by nature.

Furthermore, the very conception of change that Feuerbach seems to urge so frequently and with such emotionally charged slogans is in the last analysis understood basically as an inward change in man's consciousness, rather than as an outward transformation of nature and society. When one removes the layer of glittering phrases and vivid emotionalism, one sees that what Feuerbach is really calling on man to do is to change inwardly.[4] Man cannot change nature; he remains determined by nature.[5] But this presents no problem, for, according to Feuerbach, all that is required for man's liberation

[2] See, for example, Herbert Marcuse, *Reason and Revolution* (2nd edn.; New York: Humanities Press, 1955), pp. 270–271.

[3] *Ibid.*, p. 271.

[4] See Marx and Engels' justified critique in *The German Ideology* (New York: International Publishers, 1939), p. 37.

[5] *Ibid.*, p. 198. Cf. Marcuse, *Reason and Revolution*, pp. 271–272.

and fulfillment is an inward reorientation in man's consciousness.[6] All that is needed is for man to remove the false notion of God and the hypostatization of abstract notions and he will have achieved his liberation and realization. Man as he is and nature as it is need not be transformed; only an illusion that acts as an oppressing obstacle, that deforms man and nature, is to be removed. In the last analysis, man's realization does not come through an externally oriented action that overcomes and masters objective reality. It is an inward shift of consciousness removing an illusion. In spite of the glorious slogans, man remains inactive, inwardly oriented, and passive. He remains a passive ego.[7]

In this context, the subject, man, can no longer be conceived of exclusively as pure mind. He must be viewed whole. If man is identified with pure reason as his essence, speculative, abstract thought will once again be restored. Such an identification falsely abstracts man from his authentic, concrete reality, thus introducing again the hallmark of speculative, abstract thought. But all abstraction is false because one-sided, overlooking important and essential aspects of true reality. Feuerbach must fight the abstraction of man as reason alone, as he fought the abstraction of nature as a moment in the process of absolute mind. By the same token that nature in its true reality could not be incorporated into the process of pure reason, so man in his authentic reality cannot be absorbed into and identified with speculative reason. There is no one attribute in itself—even if it be reason—that is the true, authentic man (§ 50 below). It is a false reduction to conceive of the true man as exclusively reason. The real, concrete man is much more than his rational capacities.

> Man thinks, not the ego, not reason. . . . Man is the measure of reason. . . . Do not think as a thinker, that is, with a faculty torn from the totality of the real human being and isolated for itself;

[6] Marx, *Theses on Feuerbach,* I, II, IV, and XI. See Hook, *From Hegel to Marx,* pp. 277, 279–281, and 303–307 for further elaboration.

[7] Marx, *German Ideology,* p. 198. See Marcuse, *Reason and Revolution,* pp. 271–272.

think as a living and real being, as one exposed to the vivifying and refreshing waves of the world's oceans. Think in existence, in the world as a member of it, not in the vacuum of abstraction as a solitary monad, as an absolute monarch, as an indifferent, superworldly God. . . . (§§ 50, 51)

Man is just as much stomach as he is mind, just as much material and corporeal as he is reason and spirit. "I am a real, sensuous being and, indeed, the body in its totality is my ego, my essence itself" (§ 36).

Man is more than pure reason. He is the possessor of feelings, needs, desires, imagination, sense perception, and indeed also reason. But man's reason is not pure reason. It is reason that is determined and rectified by sense perception and the other aspects of man's being. It is reason that is only a predicate of man among the many other predicates and not the essence and substance of man. Only the total, concrete man who excludes from himself nothing essentially human can be the subject in Feuerbach's philosophy. " 'Homo sum humani nihil a me alienum puto'—this sentence, taken in its most universal and highest meaning, is the motto of the new philosophy" (§ 55).

This flesh-and-blood man in his total and concrete reality as a sensuous, feeling, desirous, imaginative being is the subject of Feuerbach's anthropological philosophy. Such a conception of man fits well into the over-all structure of Feuerbach's philosophy. It forms the proper complementary subject to the object as an independent, concrete, particular being. For such an object can be grasped, as was shown above, only in sense perception and feeling; and the subject of sense perception and feeling cannot be an abstract being of reason. It must itself be a concrete being with feeling, imagination, and sense perception. Thus, concreteness which includes all the aspects of the particular being, be it object or subject, pervades Feuerbach's thought. Feuerbach wants to grasp both subject and object in their irreducible, total, and concrete reality.

This means that Feuerbach's basic view of reality must be formulated in terms of the dualism of subject and object.

Any attempt to overcome this dualism in a monistic system based on pure thought will have to distort reality as it truly is, to abstract it from reality.

By removing pure, speculative thought from sensuous man, thus concretizing him, Feuerbach does not, however, eradicate from him the capacity to abstract. After all, man does abstract from the concreteness of given reality, and Feuerbach must account for this process in terms of sensuous man. He must further draw the distinction between those abstractions of sensuous man that are understandable and admissible and those abstractions of speculative, pure thought that are false and inadmissible. Feuerbach does this by turning to the faculty of the imagination. The imagination is an authentic aspect of sensuous man.

The objects of the imagination are sensuous. They retain their material, sensuous, and determinate qualities. Yet they are abstractions. They are not concrete objects of reality. They exist not in the external world, in reality, but in the abstracted world of fantasy. It is when the objects of the imagination are confused with the objects of sense perception, when they are substituted for them, that an offense is committed. It is in such substitution that the door is opened through which the real world can be taken into pure thought and abstracted, thus allowing man to "posit in place of the real world the imaginary and intelligible world in which there is everything that is in the real world, but abstracted and imagined" (§ 29). This is possible only because speculative thought "negates in practice the difference between imagination and perception," thus doing away with "the difference between thought and being, subjective and objective, sensuous and nonsensuous" (§ 29).

The imagination and its objects, so long as they are clearly distinguished from the real objects of sense perception, have their place in the world view of sense perception. It is here that man, to the extent that he is spontaneous, active, and creative, may express himself, since spontaneity and creativity are attributes of the imagination inasmuch as the imagination freely manipulates the data of perception and projects from them, thus creating its objects.[8] These objects of the imagination, however, have no being of their own and, therefore, are not real. They are mere creations of the imagination and belong to it. They are private and subjective. They are not part of the objective world, of reality. In the last analysis, therefore, the active aspect of the ego is merely a private, subjective aspect that creates illusions. In truth and reality, the subject of sense perception remains passive and determined. The real world is given in sense data; here, the ego is passive. Thus, the imagination, as long as its proper boundaries and nature are maintained, is not at odds with sense perception and its passive ego. On the contrary, it accommodates itself nicely to the world view of sense perception inasmuch as it accounts for the spontaneous, creative aspects of man.

It is in terms of this aspect of sensuous man, that is, of the creative aspect of the imagination, that Feuerbach understands the phenomenon of religion—an understanding that turns out to be in essence a critique of religion as traditionally understood. The commitment to sense perception as the primary organon of cognition, as the sole means by which reality is grasped, and the role assigned to the imagination in this context constitute for Feuerbach the two points that basically determine his understanding and critique of religion. Thus, his critique of religion forms an organic part of his philosophy. The commitment to sense perception as the primary organon of cognition determines his critique of religion in the same way in which it determined the other major themes of his philosophy, for example, the rejection of the reality of universals; the attack on idealistic monism and the principle of identity; the placing of reality in the object (making the subject, man, a passive recipient agent); and, finally, the resort to the subjectivity and privacy of the imagination to account for the creative aspect of man. Sense perception forms the center around which all the themes of Feuerbach's philosophy

[8] Feuerbach, *The Essence of Christianity*, trans. George Eliot (New York: Harper, 1957), pp. 29–31.

revolve and are held together in an integrated, consistent structure. Feuerbach's critique of religion, his humanization of God, exemplifies perhaps better than any other theme this basic trend and intent of Feuerbach's philosophic orientation—an orientation determined by the commitment to sense perception.

II

Feuerbach's critique of religion consists, in the main, of two arguments. In the one, Feuerbach directs his attack against the ill effects and consequences of religion in the practical, social, and material domain of human life. Religion, he claims, serves as an obstacle to man's material improvement. It is a reactionary force protecting the *status quo,* precisely because it negates the value and importance of this earthly life. In placing all its hope for salvation in Heaven and in the world to come, it disregards the misery, suffering, and injustice of this world. Life on this earth does not count. Religion leads man to accept and reconcile himself to his earthly lot of poverty and suffering by extending to him the heavenly, otherworldly vision of fulfillment and happiness. It induces day-dreaming, which hampers and interferes with the concrete work of emancipating the underprivileged and giving them their due. God is a deceit perpetuated to counteract the struggle of the underprivileged to liberate and emancipate themselves. The way to the concrete and real emancipation of the poor from material want and injustice must first go through the rejection of God. The underprivileged class, in order to liberate itself and get its due, must first become atheistic.

Feuerbach's second argument concentrates its fire in the speculative-ontological domain. Basing itself on naturalistic premises, it undertakes to deny and negate the "metaphysical correlate of faith." It undertakes to demonstrate that the full meaning and significance of the religious, metaphysical idea of God as a supernatural, independent being confronting man can be reduced to a naturalistic-anthropological idea, thus emptying the idea of the metaphysical, supernatural God of all concrete signification. The concept of the divine can now be a general concept referring to the projection and idealization of some of man's natural qualities.[1]

There are, in effect, two aspects to Feuerbach's second argument. One aspect is based directly on human experience. It is radically negative and destructive of the religious conception of God. There is no direct human experience of the supernatural God, nor is there any experience that will indicate His existence. The religious conception of God is a wishful dream and an illusion. The second aspect is an analysis of the "religious language" that religion employs. Here Feuerbach intends his analysis to be positive and constructive. He does not deny that the language of religion contains valuable and truthful insights; on the contrary, he enthusiastically affirms it. All he maintains is that it needs interpretation, it cannot be taken at face value. When taken literally, it is simply meaningless. But, when it is properly interpreted, it discloses true and penetrating insights. Feuerbach's analysis of "religious language" thus becomes a presentation of what he considers the proper interpretation of "religious language." And the one proper interpretation, according to Feuerbach, is the interpretation that refers the totality of the religious discourse exclusively to man. Man is the beginning, the middle, and the end of religious discourse. Man alone created "religious language"; he alone uses it; and he alone is the object to which it refers.

The two principal arguments are not necessarily contingent on each other. It is quite possible to agree with his first argument and at the same time reject the second. One can agree with Feuerbach—approvingly or disapprovingly—that reli-

[1] Feuerbach uses in this context the word "divine" and not "God," for the concept refers to qualities or attributes, but not to a subject. The only subject is man. "God" is a name referring to another subject which, for Feuerbach, does not exist. The word "God" is meaningless for Feuerbach. The word "divine," on the other hand, is quite meaningful.

gion has been—or, indeed, must be—a negative, conservative force in the path of social change and at the same time reject his negation of "the metaphysical correlate of faith." [2] Or one can agree with his second argument and at the same time reject his first argument. One can agree that religion is an illusion, that there is no God, and yet see in religion (that is, the illusion of religion) a dynamic force in the cause of social and economic justice.[3]

A different relation exists between the two aspects constituting the second argument. To agree with the first aspect of the argument, namely, that there is no human experience indicating the existence of God, demands agreement with the second aspect, namely, that "religious language" cannot be taken at face value, that, before it can make any sense, it must be interpreted to refer exclusively to man. To agree, however, with the second aspect of the argument, namely, that "religious language" is exclusively human discourse, does not demand agreement with the first aspect, namely, that there is no human experience indicating the existence of God. It is indeed possible to hold that there is human experience indicative of God's existence but that it is, in the last analysis, ineffable. The whole of religious discourse thus becomes man's attempt to express the inexpressible. "Religious language" is the creation of man and can be understood only as such. It expresses man, and only man. Yet, "the metaphysical correlate of faith," that is, God, is not negated.

Evidently, the weight of Feuerbach's critique lies in the first aspect of his second argument, that is, the negation of "the

[2] A good many theologians today, for example, Karl Barth, would agree with Feuerbach that religion has been historically a conservative force but would disagree with Feuerbach's rejection of "the metaphysical correlate of faith."

[3] A good instance of the latter can be seen in the movement of the Zionist-Socialists. True to their socialistic creed, they denied "the metaphysical correlate of faith" as a fantastic illusion. Yet, at the same time, they took biblical religion as their model in order to emulate its social dynamism.

metaphysical correlate of faith," the reduction of God as an independent being confronting man. Here lies the most radical challenge and threat of Feuerbach's critique, constituting as such the very center of the critique.

The reduction of God as an independent being confronting man is, however, in conformity with Feuerbach's initial commitment to the senses as the primary and determining means of human cognition and experience. Indeed, it is required by it. It is sense perception that is the stumbling block to the acceptance of "the metaphysical correlate of faith." It is sense perception, and not reason, that denies the existence of the independent, supernatural being of God. So Feuerbach's sensuous man must deny the independent, supernatural God.

There is, however, nothing new here. It is the road on which every philosopher committed to empiricism has traveled. Feuerbach is introducing nothing new to the history of religion and philosophy when he denies the existence of God.[4] "The metaphysical correlate of faith" was challenged and rejected by philosophers before him. Feuerbach's contribution lies, rather, in his explanation of how a supernatural being, independent of man and sense perception, could arise in man's consciousness. The kernel of his idea explaining the phenomenon is not really new either. Greek philosophy already had it. The impact of Feuerbach is due, however, to the extensive and thorough use he makes of it.

It is one thing to negate the existence and being of God and demonstrate their untenability, but the fact remains that people have a conception of and a belief in a supernatural being. This is just as incontestable a fact as are the facts of sense perception. Even if one grants that the notion of a supernatural God is false, how is one to account for its presence? The mere rejection of it as false is really not sufficient. One must explain the genesis of such a notion in terms of sensuous

[4] See Simon Rawidowicz, *Ludwig Feuerbachs Philosophie* (Berlin: Reuther & Reichard, 1931), pp. 209–212, for a short summary of the literature connecting Feuerbach to Xenophanes, the Sophists, Epicurus, Hume, Rousseau, Lavater, and the like.

man.[5] This is the task that Feuerbach undertakes, and he carries it out with a vengeance. Here lies his strength and the impact of his criticism of religion.

Feuerbach turns to the workings of the imagination in sensuous man in order to explain the genesis of the belief in "the metaphysical correlate of faith." He begins by introducing a psychology of projection and objectification.[6] Man projects his qualities, which are in him finite and limited, into infinity and then objectifies them, giving them an independent existence.[7] Their origin in man is forgotten, and they now confront man as independent beings. The motive power for this projection is provided by man's needs and wants which arise because of man's finite being. Projection is the mechanism that attempts to satisfy man's needs and wants by overcoming his finitude. Through projection and subsequent objectification, man creates his ideal image. He creates God. It is the human imagination that projects and is thus creative. The imagination utilizes the data given to it by sense perception as "building stones" with which it builds its creations and from which it projects its idealized images. The genesis of God is to be found in the human imagination. As pointed out before, the faculty of the imagination forms an integral part of sensuous man. It is contingent on sense perception. Thus, Feuerbach in his explanation of the genesis of the idea of God does not have recourse to factors that are not authentic, operative factors of the sensuous man. It is at this point that Feuerbach's challenge must be met by supernatural religion.

Feuerbach devotes much of his attention in his critique to the genesis of religious concepts. As a result, the faculty of man's imagination and its creative role come to occupy an important place in his works. This emphasis lends his philoso-

[5] Feuerbach, *Kritik der Hegelschen Philosophie, Sämtliche Werke,* ed. Wilhelm Bolin and Friedrich Jodl (Stuttgart: Frommanns Verlag, 1904), II, 221–222, where Feuerbach describes his method as a geneticocritical examination.

[6] *Essence of Christianity,* pp. 132, 175.

[7] *Ibid.,* p. 173.

phy a note of special interest, saving it from becoming just another run-of-the-mill sense-empirical philosophy. Sense-empirical philosophy has, by and large, failed to do justice to and concern itself with the creative aspect of man. Sensuous man is passive. The central problem is epistemological: "How can things be known to man?" In Feuerbach, one finds a sense-empirical philosophy that occupies itself with a creative aspect of man, although, in the last analysis, the validity of the creative imagination and the reality of its products are rejected. The human imagination is creative. There are no limits on the power of the imagination to create, and Feuerbach considers and analyzes the various creative aspects of the imagination at great length. His attitude toward it is, however, determined by his primary commitment to sense perception. Here lies the rub, for sense perception relegates the creative aspect of man's imagination to the realm of the fanciful. Man's creativity is not in the sphere of reality. It finds its expression, not in shaping and mastering reality, but in building castles in the air. It is a compensatory mechanism for man's wants and needs, but only in fancy and make-believe, not in truth and reality. In truth and reality, the creative aspect of the imagination can be harmful and must be rendered safe by making man aware of its unreal and fanciful nature. In truth, since its products are but dreams, religion as a product of man's creative imagination is but a dream. All that is needed to save man is to make him aware of the confusion of categories that has taken place, to open his eyes to the illusion that the products of the imagination have reality outside and independent of man.

> Religion is the dream of the human mind. But even in dreams we do not find ourselves in emptiness or in heaven, but on earth, in the realm of reality; we only see real things in the entrancing splendor of the imagination and caprice, instead of in the simple daylight of reality and necessity. Hence, I do nothing more to religion—and to speculative philosophy and theology also—than to open its eyes, or rather turn its gaze from the internal towards the external, i.e., I change the object as it is in the imagination into the object as it is in reality.[8]

[8] *Ibid.*, p. xi.

Thus, the workings of the human imagination account for the notion of God as an independent being and reality. The understanding of the psychology of the human imagination, however, destroys the notion's validity.

Eliminating God and concretizing man were for Feuerbach two sides of the same coin. The less real God is, the more real man is, and conversely. Feuerbach's reduction, however, remains in the end ambiguous. On the one hand, God is radically eliminated.[9] But, at the same time, man is not completely concretized. Feuerbach stops short of fully and completely concretizing man.[10] Sometimes he speaks of man as indeed fully concretized—as the earthly, finite human individual (§§ 52, 53 below)—but at other times he is speaking of generic man, of man in general, of the human species (§ 12). He is stopped midway in his concretization of man by his awareness of some aspects of human existence that cannot be fulfilled and realized by concrete, individual man. According to Feuerbach's understanding, the illusion of God's existence fulfilled the need of realizing man's potentialities. True, it was a realization only in imagination and therefore a mere phantom devoid of any reality. Still, it was a realization. God is the portrait that man paints of himself as fully realized.

After Feuerbach rationalizes the idea of God and demonstrates its illusory character, he must show how man's potentialities can be realized within an exclusively naturalistic and human context. This, indeed, he undertakes to do. His program is to translate the divine attributes into human attributes, to show that the divine attributes are merely the extension and fulfillment of the given human attributes.[11] With some of the attributes traditionally assigned to God, Feuerbach has no difficulty. These are the material attributes. It is conceivable and within the realm of the possible that man—concrete, individual man—should overcome hunger, pain, and poverty. If the idea of God is seen as an obstacle to

[9] *Ibid.*, pp. 38–39, 282.
[10] *Ibid.*, pp. 16, 157.
[11] *Ibid.*, p. 401; also, § 29 below.

such overcoming, then the elimination of God should open the way to the concrete, material realization of individual, particular man. So, indeed, when Feuerbach speaks of the material attributes of the divine, his man is concrete, earthly, individual man (§ 29 below).

But tradition assigned to the idea of God the realization of a class of attributes other than the material ones. One may call this class the ontological attributes: God's infinite being, eternity, omniscience, and omnipotence. These have to be, according to Feuerbach's thesis, projections from and realization of corresponding human attributes. They are the realization of the corresponding human attributes of finiteness of being, mortality, limited knowledge, and impotence.

Feuerbach is aware both of the ontological side of the traditional idea of God and of the legitimate reality of the corresponding human situation. He is aware that man has needs and wants that go beyond the material. Man's realization is not completed by giving him material happiness, namely, by removing his hunger, pain, and poverty. Man also has the need to transcend his mortality and his impotence. But how can the realization of these ontological attributes be assigned to the individual, concrete man? Surely it would not be within the naturalistic-anthropological context to suppose that the individual man could be immortal, omniscient, and omnipotent. In answer, Feuerbach introduces generic man, the human species. The man that Feuerbach now addresses is no longer the concrete individual, but man in general, the human species, past, present, and future.[12] The ontological attributes of God can be transferred to generic man. Infinity, immortality, omniscience, and unlimited power can be conceived as attributes of the human species. Thus, Feuerbach's anthropological reduction of God has this duplicity about it: the material attributes of God are reduced to the human attributes of concrete, individual man while the ontological attributes are reduced to the attributes of an abstracted, generalized concept of generic man.

[12] § 12 below; also, *Essence of Christianity*, pp. 61, 63.

An interesting point is that both those who attack Feuerbach in the defense of God and religion and those who attack him in the cause of a more thoroughgoing atheism attack him on this very point—his resort to generic man. To the former, Feuerbach's critique of religion misses the point, for he fails to appreciate the ontological predicament of the concrete, individual, single man.[13] Salvation in terms of the immortality of the species is no salvation for the concrete individual who is concerned with his finiteness and the fact that he must die. To the latter, Feuerbach, despite all his protestations against religion, remains nevertheless within the religious sphere. They equate religion with abstraction; and, to them, a generalized concept is a religious concept.[14] Since Feuerbach, so they argue, did not really free himself from abstraction and generalization in his conception of man, he remains within the sphere of religion. Thus, Feuerbach is found lacking by critics from both the right and the left, his conception of the generic man affording the focal point of the critiques directed against him.

Feuerbach's critique hit the German philosophical-theological community of the 1840's like a thunderbolt. As David Friedrich Strauss once remarked, the decade belonged to Feuerbach. But, like a thunderbolt, he soon passed into oblivion. Only after World War I does Feuerbach return, slowly but surely, to gain attention among those interested in religion and philosophical anthropology. His return has not been nearly so meteoric as his first appearance was. More serious attention, however, seems to be accorded to what he has to say, and the indications are that he will also stay with us for a longer while than was the case in the nineteenth century. Feuerbach's critique of religion commands a new attention in our day, and its impact is pervasive. This is understandable in

[13] Karl Barth, *Protestant Thought*, trans. B. Cozens, rev. trans. H. H. Hartnell (New York: Harper, 1959), pp. 360–361. See also his introductory eassy to *Essence of Christianity*, pp. xxviii–xxix.

[14] Marx, *Theses on Feuerbach*, IV, VI, VII. See also Hook, *From Hegel to Marx*, p. 223.

terms of the position from which the critique is launched, the premises on which it is built, and the interests it comes to defend. The more these are in accord with the spirit of the age, the more telling and forceful will be the impact of the critique. And Feuerbach's critique is based on a position that is closely akin to the spirit of our age. In the two arguments constituting his critique, Feuerbach gives expression to some of the most pervasive features of the contemporary world, and many will wholeheartedly agree with the premises on which his critique is based.

Feuerbach's first argument against religion issues from his cry for social and economic justice, more specifically, from his demand to give the worker his due. He closely binds his critique to the cause of the underprivileged. He pits God against the poor, religion against economic justice, and theology against social progress. Certainly, in our time, more than ever before, we have become aware of the just claim of the working man to receive his due. No longer can we find it within ourselves to justify the poverty, misery, and oppression of the underprivileged. No longer can we remain insensitive to economic injustice and exploitation. And the working man himself has reached, in our age, self-consciousness demanding his rightful place under the sun. He has raised his voice and made his existence known. Feuerbach, in making his critique part of the struggle for economic emancipation and social liberation, is thus authentically speaking for our age.

The first aspect of Feuerbach's second argument is based on naturalistic and anthropocentric premises. In both his anthropocentrism and his naturalism, he is addressing modern man on the wavelength to which he is best attuned. Man is the center of our concern and interest. The rise of the social sciences, of psychology, and particularly of philosophical anthropology indicates this clearly. Feuerbach's anthropologizing of religion thus appeals cogently to the modern mind and temper. Religion, like every other cultural manifestation, is to be understood as the creation of man's spirit. Its source is man, and, similarly, the object to which religion refers is also man.

Only in such terms can modern man grasp religion. But, not only is man the center of our attention, he is also the ultimate criterion of what is acceptable and what is not acceptable. Modern man is truly "the measure of all things." No other measure is admitted. He will submit to no higher authority. Modern man is not incapable of listening but unwilling to listen to anything beyond himself. He can give, but not receive. Closely connected with this anthropocentric orientation is a thoroughgoing naturalism. Modern man cannot but regard every vestige of supernaturalism—be it with regard to himself or to the world—as absurd, fantastic, and superstitious. Only the categories of naturalism are accepted in the interpretation of man and his experience of the world. Naturalism and anthropocentrism are the distinctive marks of the temper of modern man, and Feuerbach's critique embeds itself deeply in both.

In the second aspect of his second argument, Feuerbach resorts to a method that would be most congenial to the mind of contemporary philosophers. His critique is directed against the language of religion. He clearly detects in language the locus of meaning, and his critique is really a critique in semantics. The whole of his critique can be reduced to the question: "Which part of speech is the word 'God'? Is it properly a noun or an adjective?" Feuerbach is primarily concerned with the meaning and significance of religious statements. Their truth content is only secondary. Feuerbach's critique nowhere deals with "natural" or "rational" theology, that is, with the validity of theological proofs for the existence of God. His is not a critique of the epistemological or logical validity of the *quinque viae,* as Hume's critique in the *Dialogues Concerning Natural Religion* was, or, indeed, as most philosophical critiques of theology have been. Feuerbach, in shifting the discussion to the domain of language analysis and in raising the questions of meaning and significance, is breaking new ground in the dialogue between philosophy and religion. As such, his critique and analysis of "religious language" is contemporaneous with the most recent discussions in philosophical theology.

He would have fitted comfortably into the company of the philosophers and theologians who produced the volumes *Faith and Logic* and *New Essays in Philosophical Theology.*

Thus, Feuerbach's critique in all its aspects attacks religion from positions that express authentic and pervasive trends in the cultural consciousness of our age. Hence, his critique can no longer be seen as the mere expression of an individual—be he ever so penetrating and decisive in his insights—but must be taken as an important voice of our cultural milieu. It is by virtue of this position, that is, the expression of an important orientation of contemporary cultural consciousness, that the critique exercises its strong impact and occupies such a central place in contemporary apologetics.

III

How did Feuerbach arrive at a philosophy based on sense perception? After all, his philosophic origins lie in a tradition alien to empiricism. His philosophic training and, so to speak, upbringing were in the idealistic tradition; his teacher was Hegel, not Hume. Furthermore, not only was Feuerbach a student of Hegelian idealism, he accepted it and was one of its spokesmen.

It is often overlooked that Feuerbach was for about fifteen years—from about 1824, when he first came under Hegel's influence, to 1839—an ardent disciple of Hegel, a true, undeviating Hegelian.[1] From his dissertation, *De ratione, una universali, infinita,* in 1828, through his anonymously published *Gedanken über Tod und Unsterblichkeit* in 1830, the *Satyrisch-Theologischen Distichen* (1830), *Abälard und Heloise,* his critique of Carl Bachmann's *Anti-Hegel* in 1835, his histories of philosophy, *From Bacon to Spinoza* (1833), *Leibniz* (1836), and *Pierre Bayle* (1838), to his *Zur Kritik der Hegelschen Philosophie* in 1839, the master whom Feuerbach

[1] Rawidowicz rightly makes this point in his *Ludwig Feuerbachs Philosophie,* p. 15, *contra* Wilhelm Bolin's *Ludwig Feuerbach, Sein Wirken und Seine Zeitgenossen* (Stuttgart: Frommanns Verlag, 1891), p. 70.

follows, identifies with, and so vigorously defends is Hegel. In his dissertation, he keeps the Hegelian threefold division of treating, first, pure thought; second, the thought that thinks itself; and, third, the synthesis of the two. He asserts the complete identity of thought and being and of spirit and thought.[2] The *Vernunft* is infinite, and it includes nature.[3] It is the essential reality. Man is man only insofar as he is spirit, and spirit is spirit only insofar as it is thought.[4] The complete, absolute unity of "I" and "thou" is to be found, not in love, but in thought. His philosophy throughout is a monistic, speculative, idealistic system in which *Vernunft* reigns supreme.

In the *Gedanken,* we have the speculative, idealistic comprehension and solution of the religious problem.[5] Nature is grasped as the otherness of God, who is unlimited in both time and space.[6] Time and space are understood in a speculative-mystical fashion that is akin to pantheism.[7] Man's vocation is not to act, but to remember the happenings that are eternal, to convert the deeds of being to deeds of thought and self-consciousness. Sense perception is not "the Truth," but merely a passage to reason, which is being in itself, timeless activity, and the perceiving of the whole.[8] Only the universal, the whole, the absolute can be complete and perfect. The universal is the only reality and essential being, whereas the subjective individual is lacking, negative, and finite; individuals are limits and fetters.[9] The highest life is the life lived in the universal idea—in religion, science, and art.[10] In his critique of Bachmann, he strongly defends the concept of identity, particularly the identity of logic and metaphysics.[11] He vigor-

[2] *De ratione,* p. 4.
[3] *Ibid.,* pp. 21, 28.
[4] *Ibid.,* p. 31.
[5] *Sämtliche Werke,* III, 17–18.
[6] *Ibid.,* p. 29.
[7] *Ibid.,* pp. 39, 57.
[8] *Ibid.,* pp. 48, 54, 74.
[9] *Ibid.,* p. 57.
[10] *Ibid.,* pp. 76–77.
[11] *Ibid.,* II, 25, 28.

ously attacks—under the influence of speculative philosophy —Bachmann's empiricism as blind perception.[12] In the defense of extreme panlogical idealism, he attacks all forms of materialism. Philosophy and thought, he exclaims, are not dependent on eating and drinking.[13] In his historical works, great attention is given the rational idealistic systems, whereas hardly any is accorded the sensualistic, materialistic philosophies. Hobbes and Gassendi are sharply rejected. English empiricism is hardly mentioned. On the other hand, Spinoza, Leibniz, and even Böhme play important roles. Spinoza is understood in Hegel's spirit of the panlogical dialectic. It is the pure, absolute, independent philosophy.[14] No other philosophical figure except Hegel receives such high praise from Feuerbach as does Leibniz. Feuerbach fully defends Leibniz' opposition to Locke's empiricism, which he sees as "superficial." The empiricist commits the mistake of converting a condition into a cause, and spirit, which is the active agent, into a passive recipient. The senses illuminate the world for us, but the light is not their own. It comes from the central sun of the spirit. All true philosophy is speculative idealism.[15]

It seems clear that, until 1839, Feuerbach is a thoroughgoing disciple of Hegel, attacking the very position he was later to assume. There is a radical turn in Feuerbach's philosophical orientation. One can say that, until 1839, Hegel determines Feuerbach's thought positively, as the unquestioned master to be followed. After 1839, Hegel continues to determine Feuerbach's thought, but as the enemy to be destroyed.

The change in Feuerbach came about in two stages. The initial break between Feuerbach and Hegel appeared, interestingly enough, in their understanding of religion. This, in turn, led to the total break between them as expressed in their

[12] *Ibid.*, p. 54.
[13] *Ibid.*, p. 55.
[14] *Ibid.*, IV, 327; V, 259–269.
[15] *Ibid.*, 61, 83, 122–125.

respective conceptions of philosophy. Once the break in the realm of religion occurred, it was inevitable that a total break in the realm of philosophy would follow, for their religion was religious anthropology as, indeed, their philosophy was philosophical anthropology.

In the mid-1830's, Feuerbach, still an ardent follower of Hegel, was already taking a different, negative approach to the question of religion and theology. He was able to maintain this double relationship to Hegel only by having first challenged Hegel's identification of philosophy and religion. Feuerbach at this time separates the two, so that, while maintaining his adherence to Hegelian speculative idealism, he can at the same time launch his attack against religion and theology. Already at the end of his *Leibniz* he attempts to show that reason and faith, philosophy and theology, can never be united.[16] This is stated even more explicitly in his *Bayle*. Feuerbach strongly identifies himself with Bayle, whom he sees as the true philosopher in all matters concerning theology, for in such matters Bayle was a skeptic. Science and philosophy are the symbols of reason, whereas faith operates in the sphere of unreason and the unnatural. Faith belongs to the realm of will—the arbitrary and the lawless. Any mediation of dogmatics and philosophy is a false concordat that should be protested against in the name of both religion and philosophy. Accordingly, as there is no Christian medicine or mathematics, so also there should be no Christian philosophy.

Feuerbach fights for the freedom and independence of philosophy from religion, for he understands religion to lie outside the sphere of reason.[17] Religion is not accessible to reason. It differs from philosophy, not only in form, but in essence. Here lies a fundamental break with Hegel. Hegel maintains that the content of religion and philosophy is the same and that they differ only in their form, philosophy expressing itself in ideas, religion expressing itself in sensuous symbols. But,

16 *Ibid.*, 176–181.

17 See, for example, *ibid.*, VII, 197–198.

Feuerbach argues, Hegel's very principle of the inseparability of matter and form negates this unity of content. The sensuous form of the religious symbol will therefore determine the content of religion, thus differentiating it from the content of philosophy whose form is the idea. Both the content and form of religion are contingent on sense. Thus, Feuerbach's initial break with Hegel consists in the transfer of religion from the sphere of thought to that of feeling. Feuerbach follows here Novalis and the romantics in conceiving religion as a subject matter of the heart and not of the mind.[18] "Religion is only an affection, feeling, heart, love." [19] Religion does not appeal to man's reason, but to his feelings, to his desire for happiness.

This new direction in his understanding of religion brings Feuerbach into close association with the pietistic and romantic trends of German philosophy. This is a position at the opposite pole from Hegel's and one that Hegel strongly attacks. For Hegel, feeling is the lowest form and the least satisfactory vehicle in which to convey the content of religion. Of course, religion as a spiritual content, as a content of consciousness, may find expression in feeling, but it is a poor expression. In feeling, man is not distinguished from the animal. Expression in feeling leads to subjectivity and hence to complete arbitrariness.[20]

> As soon as a content enters feeling, then everyone is reduced to his subjective viewpoint. . . .Thus, one can say that he has religion in feeling and another can say that he cannot find God in feeling, and each will be right. If the divine content—the divine revelation, the relation of man to God, the being of God for man—is reduced in this manner to mere feeling, so it will be limited to the viewpoint of special subjectivity, arbitrariness, and favor.[21]

[18] Rawidowicz, *Ludwig Feuerbachs Philosophie,* p. 93. Also, *Essence of Christianity,* p. 186.

[19] *Sämtliche Werke,* II, 260.

[20] Karl Löwith, *Von Hegel zu Nietzsche* (Stuttgart: W. Kohlhammer, 1941), p. 355.

[21] Hegel, *Die Vernunft in der Geschichte,* Introduction to *Vorlesungen über die Philosophie der Geschichte,* ed. G. Lasson (Leipzig: F. Meiner, 1920), p. 20.

Quite clearly, Hegel could see the consequences that would follow. He therefore rejects the alternative of placing religion in feeling. Feuerbach does not follow him here. He recognizes that religion cannot be a matter of the mind or intellect alone. For Feuerbach, religion in its quest for personal happiness must be a manifestation of feeling.[22] But, of course, the consequences, as Hegel saw them, had to follow.

For Feuerbach, the implications of this separation of religion grounded in feelings from philosophy based on reason are far-reaching. They push beyond merely maintaining the independence of religion from philosophy. In the context of absolute idealism, one cannot stop at this point. By placing religion in the sphere of emotion, one undermines the universality of reason. Here is an area of human experience not subject to reason. The system of reason is damaged. The Hegelian system can hardly afford to recognize an exception without abdicating its claim to universality. And the claim to universality is the very essence of the Hegelian system.

The position that Feuerbach was maintaining in the late 1830's, that of being a Hegelian idealist and yet at the same time excluding religion from the system of reason,[23] was by its very nature precarious. A lasting balance could not be struck at this point. With Feuerbach, the scale tilted toward

[22] Seeing religion in the domain of feeling places Feuerbach in close proximity to people like Lavater, Novalis, and particularly Schleiermacher. Schleiermacher must have had a strong influence on Feuerbach, providing the emotional, anthropocentric basis for the understanding of religion that served Feuerbach as the initial and decisive point of departure from Hegel. (See Feuerbach's reminiscences of his student days in Berlin, *Ausgewählte Briefe,* ed. W. Bolin [Leipzig: Frommanns Verlag, 1904], I, 176 ff.)

But despite the closeness of Schleiermacher's and Feuerbach's understanding of religion as grounded in human emotions and man's self-consciousness, their further understanding of religion and, indeed, their intentions are quite different. For a treatment of the relationship between Feuerbach and Schleiermacher, see Rawidowicz, *Ludwig Feuerbachs Philosophie,* pp. 189–192.

[23] Rawidowicz, *Ludwig Feuerbachs Philosophie,* pp. 61–62, 65–66.

sense perception and emotion and against absolute reason. The crevice that was made in speculative idealism by excluding religion from its domain was widened into an all-encompassing abyss which swallowed speculative philosophy in its entirety. Philosophy, however, is again identified with religion, now no longer on the basis of reason, but on that of sense perception (§ 64 below). In the same way, theology is identified with speculative philosophy, and both are now rejected (§§ 18, 23). Both religion and philosophy are to be cleansed, the former by removal of its theological elements, the latter, by eradication of its speculative-metaphysical ones. The scale is now tilted in favor of empiricism and against idealism. Feuerbach's viewpoint is now empirical-naturalistic, not only with regard to religion, but also with regard to philosophy. From now on, he can proceed to attack theology and, thus, speculative idealism.

IV

The question of Feuerbach's relation to Hegel has received new nuances in the literature as a result of the "discovery" of Hegel's early writings. It was Wilhelm Dilthey who called attention in 1905, in his important book *Jugendgeschichte Hegels,* to Hegel's early philosophy. In 1907, Herman Nohl, who was Dilthey's student, edited and published some of Hegel's unpublished writings from the years 1795 to 1800 under the title *Hegels theologische Jugendschriften.* In 1923, Georg Lasson edited and published the notes of lectures on logic, metaphysics, and natural philosophy that Hegel delivered at the University of Jena. And, in 1931 and 1932, J. Hoffmeister edited and published the Jena lecture notes on *Realphilosophie.* The latter writings are known as the Jenenser System and cover the years 1802–1806. These writings, both the early theological writings and the Jenenser System, reveal new aspects of Hegel's thought. They have given rise to new interpretations of Hegel's significance, particularly with reference to the development of his thought. We need not discuss here the question of whether these writings are, as Richard Kroner maintains,[1] to be interpreted as stages in Hegel's development leading to and culminating in the later, post-*Phenomenology* Hegel or whether they constitute, as Herbert Marcuse maintains,[2] a position against which Hegel's later writings signify a radical break. The "discovery" of these Hegelian writings, however, gave rise also to interpretations linking Feuerbach to the early Hegel[3] and suggest an identity of thought between the two. What these interpretations basically maintain is that Feuerbach contributed nothing essentially new, that what Feuerbach says Hegel already knew and, indeed, had advanced beyond it.

But it is abundantly clear that Feuerbach had no inkling of Hegel's early unpublished writings. None of the post-Hegelians, with the exception of Karl Rosenkranz and Rudolf Haym, knew the early Hegel. Therefore, the Hegel that Feuerbach knows and to whom he relates is exclusively the later, post-*Phenomenology* Hegel. The only question is whether Feuerbach resorts unknowingly to a position that was already maintained by the early Hegel.

Hegel's treatment of the question of religion generally and Christianity specifically in his early theological writings discloses a number of motives that at first glance resemble Feuerbach's basic orientation in his treatment of religion. Thus we meet in the fragment on "Volksreligion und Christentum" the emotional viewpoint as the center of his reflections on religion. Religion is not mere knowledge of God and the relationship of man and the world to him. It is not a mere historical or rational knowledge. The essence of religion lies, rather, in the fact that it involves and influences our heart.

[1] "Hegel's Philosophical Development," in T. M. Knox, trans., Hegel, *Early Theological Writings* (Chicago: University of Chicago Press, 1948), pp. 34, 43–44.

[2] Marcuse, *Reason and Revolution,* pp. ix, 92, 96.

[3] See, for example, Rawidowicz, *Ludwig Feuerbachs Philosophie,* pp. 225, 227, 228; Löwith, *Von Hegel zu Nietzsche,* p. 351.

Religion is a matter of the heart.[4] . . . When I speak of religion I remove myself from all scientific or, even more, from all metaphysical knowledge of God and of our and the world's relation to him. Such knowledge in which only the mere rationalizing understanding is involved is theology but no longer religion.[5] . . . Religion is for the heart and wants to be for the heart.[6] . . . When I say that a man has religion, it does not mean that he has much knowledge of religion, but rather that his heart feels the acts, the wonder, and the closeness of the divine.[7]

Hegel is here learning his lessons from Greek folk religion, interpreting it in the light of Herder's ideas. It is a religion of enthusiasm and the imagination.[8] Religion concerns the individual. It is not objective; it is the concern of the subjective individual. The theme of love as the foundation of religion also appears here.

God is love, and love is God. There is no other divinity than love—only that which is not divine, which does not love, must have the divine outside itself in the idea.[9] . . . Religion is the same as love. That which is loved is not standing apart and against us, but is one with our essence; we see only ourselves in it.[10]

Such utterances only naturally bring Feuerbach to mind.

Feuerbach, we have seen, also understands religion in terms of the emotions, the individual, subjectivity, and love. But this is not to say that Feuerbach and the early Hegel are identical or that Feuerbach has nothing new to say. The crucial point is not that both Feuerbach and the early Hegel are using the same basic concepts in their reflections on religion. This actually should not be so surprising. Hegel in his young manhood "was an enthusiastic Romanticist." [11] He knew the representative thinkers of *Sturm und Drang*, Jacobi, Herder,

[4] *Hegels theologische Jugendschriften*, ed. Herman Nohl (Tübingen: J. C. B. Mohr, 1907), p. 10.

[5] *Ibid.*, p. 8.

[6] *Ibid.*, p. 11.

[7] *Ibid.*, p. 6.

[8] Kroner, "Hegel's Philosophical Development," p. 3.

[9] *Theologische Jugendschriften*, p. 391.

[10] *Ibid.*, pp. 377–378.

[11] Kroner, "Hegel's Philosophical Development," p. 14.

Hamann, and the spokesmen for romanticism, Novalis, Hölderlin, Friedrich Schlegel, and, of course, Schelling, the philosopher of romanticism.[12] Feuerbach, too, when he breaks away in the mid-1830's from the later Hegel's treatment of religion, is turning to romanticism for his understanding of religion. Emotions, the individual, subjectivity, and love are common concepts of romanticism that neither Feuerbach nor the early Hegel can claim as his own contribution.

The crucial question in discussing Feuerbach's relation to the early Hegel is therefore not whether there is similarity in many aspects of their thought, but what they do with their original romantic conception of religion. Here Feuerbach is moving in a different direction altogether from that of Hegel. For Hegel, the romantic emphasis on the emotions is just a stage, a reaction against the narrow and one-sided view of rationalism that was the heritage of the Enlightenment and that he himself maintained before.[13] His underlying concern and quest is to find the principle by which absolute unity and the reconciliation of all opposites can be achieved. He is in search of a way by which "the Whole and the Parts, the Universe and the Particular Objects, the Infinite and the Finite, the Unlimited and the Limited are united in the Whole, the Universe, the Infinite."[14] Romanticism is for Hegel an experiment to see whether this pantheistic unity can be achieved through the emotions alone. When it is abandoned, it is because he believes that he has found his solution in yet another principle that transcends and yet includes as stages both the narrow reason of the Enlightenment and the emotions of romanticism. Hegel gratified his romantic longing for unity in the unromantic principle of a higher reason and "a logic of life."[15] His romanticism was a stage that led to the absolute unity of being and thought in *Geist,* in the higher life of the spirit.

[12] *Ibid.,* pp. 3, 11, 15, 16, 20.
[13] *Ibid.,* pp. 8, 12, 14.
[14] *Ibid.,* p. 13.
[15] *Ibid.,* pp. 15, 31.

For Feuerbach, on the other hand, the romantic emphasis on the emotions led, as we have shown, to an anthropology based on sense perception and a thoroughgoing naturalism. The road to Hegel's "mystical pantheism," as Dilthey calls it,[16] was closed to Feuerbach, for his conception of being would never have allowed the absolute identity of being and thought. The romantic principle of the emotions signals for Feuerbach the break with Hegelian monism and its principle of reconciliation in absolute mind. It pointed toward a dualistic *Weltanschauung* where an irreducible object confronts the subject. It led Feuerbach in an opposite direction, one that Hegel, at all periods of his philosophy, would have considered very one-sided and unsatisfactory. This different "pointing" that the romantic principle had for Hegel and Feuerbach was not accidental but basic to their philosophic orientations and intentions. So, although the early Hegel and Feuerbach meet at the point of their respective associations with romanticism, their ways necessarily lead in opposite directions. This should be stressed against those who want to see a simple identity of and continuation between Feuerbach and the early Hegel. There is more that separates than unites.

A similar objection must be raised against the attempts to link Feuerbach to the Hegel of the Jenenser System. Again, no claim is made that Feuerbach knew the Jena Hegel, but it is maintained that unknowingly Feuerbach proceeded in the philosophic trend of the Jena Hegel.

Marcuse sees a definite break occurring in Hegel's thought that radically differentiates the later Hegel from the Jena one. The Jena Hegel is deeply involved in the political, social, and economic aspects of human life.[17] In this context, man is seen as the active agent who—as a self-reliant master of his life—can control and direct change.[18] Man is not the passive, deter-

[16] Wilhelm Dilthey, *Gesammelte Schriften*, Vol. IV, *Jugendgeschichte Hegels* (Leipzig: B. G. Teubner, 1921), p. 154.

[17] *Reason and Revolution*, pp. 11, 16, 29, 31, 77.

[18] *Ibid.*, p. 6.

mined being propelled by the cosmic process. He is given power to shape the world and bring about its realization.[19] The present world is alienated from its true reality and in bondage. It is a world of disunity and disintegration, a world full of contradiction.[20] Its realization can, therefore, be achieved only by negating and overcoming its present institutions and conditions. The Jenenser System is thus a negative and critical philosophy.[21] It is a revolutionary call on man to do something about his alienated self and his estranged world.[22] Existence is a life-and-death struggle, and man is called on to partake actively in its struggle, to revolutionize its *status quo,* and to direct its outcome.[23] The outcome is not predetermined. The future is open; it depends on what man will or will not do. And the matrix for man's actions is history.[24] History is thus the central category in the Jenenser System. It is concrete, open-ended history whose course is a true life-and-death struggle, a mortal combat. Historical and social action are now pointed to as the realization and thus also the negation of philosophy. "The truth now would require actual historical practice to fulfill it." [25]

Marcuse contends that the later Hegel turned pessimistic and lost his confidence in the eventual realization of his ideal in concrete history. Reality appears to him now to offer "no adequate fulfillment of the proper potentialities of men and things." [26] He retreats from the concrete, historical world into the inner life of the spirit to find there fulfillment and realization.[27] He abandons the French Revolution and returns to his

19 *Ibid.,* pp. 39, 97.
20 *Ibid.,* pp. 25, 35, 49, 65, 113.
21 *Ibid.,* pp. 27, 64.
22 *Ibid.,* p. 51.
23 *Ibid.,* p. 100.
24 *Ibid.,* pp. ix, 99.
25 *Ibid.,* p. 28.
26 *Ibid.,* p. 42.
27 *Ibid.,* p. 92.

age-old native German tradition of the Lutheran Reformation that taught that "liberty was an 'inner value' which was compatible with every form of bondage." [28] In such a context,

> Social reality became inconsequential as far as the true essence of man was concerned. Man learned to turn on himself his demand for the satisfaction of his potentialities and "to seek within" himself, not in the outer world, his life's fulfillment.[29]

We encounter here a Hegel who is preoccupied with the inner realm of the idea, who is above and beyond the concrete and mortal struggles of history. He is the owl of Minerva, the calm metaphysician standing at the end of history contemplating and looking back merely in order to understand and explain the totality of experience.[30]

Feuerbach would appear, in this context, to be the Hegel who did not become pessimistic about the prospects of man's concrete realization. Far from being pessimistic, he is exuberant in his conviction that mankind has reached maturity and is at the point of realizing itself.[31] He proclaims loudly and clearly that the means are at hand to transform and liberate mankind.[32] "Hegel's great error was that he stuck to idealism at a time when a materialistic solution of the problem was at hand." [33] Feuerbach thus appears to be a continuation of the Jena Hegel. What the Jena Hegel merely alluded to, namely, the negation of philosophy and its culmination in social action, Feuerbach asserts fully and without qualifications. He is a "Jena Hegel" who remains an optimist and hence does not succumb to idealism.

It seems difficult, however, to connect Feuerbach to the Jena Hegel. There are two basic features of Feuerbach's philosophy that are in contradiction to the Jena Hegel. First, for Feuerbach, nature is the domain where man is to realize himself.[34] It is nature that basically determines and conditions

[28] *Ibid.*, p. 14.
[29] *Ibid.*, p. 14.
[30] *Ibid.*, pp. 93, 120.
[31] *Ibid.*, p. 267.
[32] *Ibid.*, p. 268.
[33] *Ibid.*, p. 268.
[34] Feuerbach, *Vorläufige Thesen*, in *Sämtliche Werke*, II, 263.

human existence and in which, correspondingly, man is to find his realization. Human existence is primarily natural existence. In the Jena Hegel, on the other hand, the matrix of human existence is history and society, and, correspondingly, they are the media of man's realization.[35] Human existence is primarily social and historical existence. Nature is brought into the historical and social matrix through the process of labor.[36] Only in the context of the labor process, which is fundamentally a social relation between man and man, does nature play a role, and at that a relatively unimportant role. Whereas the analysis of the labor process is fundamental in the Jena Hegel, it is of absolutely no concern or interest to Feuerbach. Whereas the Jena Hegel conceives of man's realization through the social and historical processes of labor, "Feuerbach, *per contra,* introduces nature as the basis and medium for liberating mankind. Philosophy is negated and fulfilled by nature." [37]

Second, Feuerbach sees man as a passive agent. Man's basic attribute is "suffering"; man is primarily a receptive and determined being.[38]

> Man's suffering is a "natural" relation of the living subject to its objective environment, for the subject is opposed and overwhelmed by the object. Nature shapes and determines the ego from without, making it essentially "passive." The process of liberation cannot eliminate this passivity.[39]

Man in the Jena Hegel is, on the other hand, an active, spontaneous, self-determining agent. Man is given the power to direct his historical destiny and determine the social relations of his environment.

It is clear that Feuerbach cannot be understood as a continuation of the Jena Hegel who remained optimistic and thus

35 Hegel, *Jenenser Realphilosophie,* ed. J. Hoffmeister (Leipzig: F. Meiner, 1932), I, 215–240.

36 See Marcuse, *Reason and Revolution,* pp. 109–118.

37 *Ibid.,* p. 270.

38 § 32 below; also *Vorläufige Thesen,* p. 253.

39 Marcuse, *Reason and Revolution,* pp. 270–271.

proceeded to negate philosophy in the name of materialism. A much more fundamental difference in orientation divides Feuerbach from the Jena Hegel than that of optimism versus pessimism.

Such attempts to relate Feuerbach to the Hegel of the *Early Theological Writings* or to the Hegel of the *Jenenser System* must be rejected. Feuerbach's thought is moving in a fundamentally different direction. This objection would apply also to a further attempt whereby Feuerbach is seen as the continuation and culmination of the later Hegel or other predecessors. Such an interpretation would maintain that the whole trend of German philosophy and theology is leading to Feuerbach. It lays the premise that makes Feuerbach's "unwelcome conclusion" unavoidable.[40] The line of development leading to and culminating in Feuerbach is the theme of man's apotheosis which is being proclaimed with ever-increasing consistency and clarity. It reaches new heights in Hegel and culminates in Feuerbach. The apotheosis of man forms the foundation of both Hegel's and Feuerbach's philosophies. It is in this sense that Feuerbach is but the continuation of Hegel.

The thing to note here, however, is that the theme of man's apotheosis has two aspects. First, it signifies the closing of the gap between the divine and the human. The "wholly other" aspect of the divine is abolished. The duality of God and man is nullified. To the extent that this aspect is present in the phenomenon of man's apotheosis in pre-Feuerbachian German philosophy and theology, Feuerbach can be seen as, in a sense, "the point of intersection where all these lines converge." Indeed, Feuerbach's position becomes a threat to theology whenever "mystical ideas of the union of God and man" are employed in theology.[41] Second, man's apotheosis also signifies that the duality of God and man, the gap between them, is reduced in God's direction. The phenomenon of human apotheosis raises man to the divine. It is man become God.

40 Barth, *Protestant Thought,* p. 358.
41 *Ibid.,* pp. 358–359.

This may be the case with Hegel, but not with Feuerbach. With Feuerbach, the reduction takes place in the opposite direction. It is God who is reduced to man (§§ 1 and 52 below). It is God become man. One witnesses in Feuerbach the humanization of God, not the apotheosis of man. Thus, Feuerbach cannot be seen as the continuation and culmination of Hegel, although for Christian theology, which maintains a delicate balance of the duality of God and man, the basic concern is the tipping of the balance regardless of the direction, and both Hegel and Feuerbach tipped the balance. The fact remains, however, that Feuerbach is tipping the balance in the direction opposite to that of Hegel.

The same distinction can be made with regard to the contention that Feuerbach continues the themes of fetishism and alienation that originate in Hegel. The cause of alienation can be conceived in more than one way. Alienation can be understood as man's condition caused by the fact that man, whose true nature is divine, falls short of the divine in his actual existence. To the extent that man has not realized himself as divine, he is estranged from his true, authentic self. This may well be Hegel's understanding of alienation. But alienation can also be understood as man's condition caused by the fact that man projects part of his being into another imaginary being. To the extent that man has part of his being torn away from him, he is estranged from his full, complete being. This is Feuerbach's understanding of alienation.[42] With Hegel, therefore, the cause of alienation is that man does not realize himself as God. With Feuerbach, the cause is that man has a fantasy of a God.[43] Correspondingly, the overcoming of alienation consists for the later Hegel in a transcending of the limitation of space and time so that thinking man can comprehend and be the totality of all reality, whereas for Feuerbach the overcoming of alienation consists in the removal of all traces of transcendence and the supernatural, reducing

[42] *Essence of Christianity*, pp. 26, 33, 73, 196.

[43] See Robert Tucker, *Philosophy and Myth in Karl Marx* (New York: Cambridge University Press, 1961), p. 92.

man fully and completely to space and time (§ 44 below). An interpretation of Feuerbach as a direct continuation of the later Hegel is therefore unacceptable.

I have tried to show briefly that the various formulations that would view Feuerbach as a continuation of Hegel, be it the early Hegel, the Jena Hegel or the later Hegel, although they are suggestive and intriguing and no doubt shed some light on important aspects of the relationship, still in the last analysis fail to represent truly the essential relationship between Feuerbach and Hegel. They all miss or minimize the essential and basic aspect of Feuerbach's mature philosophic position (post 1839), namely, that it is a position based on sense perception. As such, it introduces, despite many similarities, a basic difference with the early, romantic Hegel and finds itself in a different context altogether from the Jena Hegel, with his primacy of the historical category and the labor conflict, and even further away from the later Hegel. We must accept, therefore, the old view—and the one that is also prima facie the most obvious—whereby Feuerbach is seen as the archrebel and attacker of the position of the later Hegel. This is the only Hegel he knows, and after 1839 the prima facie burden of Feuerbach's philosophy lies, aside from the critique of religion, in a consistent attack on the philosophic position of the later Hegel, which is indeed equated with the position of religion. Thus, one can say, at least on prima facie evidence, that after 1839 all of Feuerbach's philosophical efforts are directed against the position of the later Hegel.

The recent trend to maintain that what came after Hegel (therefore including Feuerbach) is already stated in Hegel and indeed in a much better way, oversimplifies matters (certainly with regard to Feuerbach). Surely, Feuerbach's sense empiricism and naturalistic anthropology based on sense perception are not to be found in Hegel at any time, nor, indeed, is it to be found in the mainstream of German philosophy generally. Feuerbach is essentially a lonely figure, not only regarding his predecessors, but also, as we shall see later, regarding his contemporaries with whom also he may share similarities. The similarities, however, never touch the essence of his position. Essentially, he is alone. He is a sense empiricist in the midst of a metaphysical-idealistic tradition. And the relation here between these two positions must be one of opposition. Thus, Feuerbach's opposition to the later Hegel is not only supported by the prima facie evidence of Feuerbach's writings but must be understood as an essential and necessary consequence of these two positions. This must have been apparent in the presentation (Section I above) of the thematic structure of Feuerbach's philosophic position. Although the intention was to present Feuerbach's philosophy in its own terms, it was not possible to do so without a continuous comparison and critique of the metaphysical-idealistic position. This, indeed, is also the case with Feuerbach. Even in that part of the *Principles* that is devoted to the positive formulation of his philosophy, Feuerbach continually returns to his critique of the metaphysical-idealistic position. It would seem that he can formulate his position only in the process of attacking and criticizing the other.

Although the basic contour of Feuerbach's critique could have already been detected in the treatment of Part I, I shall now review and enlarge the treatment of the critique, for it forms an essential part of Feuerbach's relation to the later Hegel and, indeed, to the whole metaphysical-idealistic tradition that for Feuerbach started as far back as neo-Platonism.

Feuerbach understands Hegel as the culmination of the neo-Platonic spirit which pervades the whole of the idealistic tradition of the modern world. The Hegelian contribution is to have rationalized neo-Platonism. "That which is imagination and fantasy with the neo-Platonists was merely rationalized and transformed into concepts by Hegel."[44] The basic neo-Platonic orientation, which Hegel merely attempted to express in rational and conceptual terms, is to have denied matter an independent reality. The totality of reality is idea and thought. Ancient Greek philosophy, as formulated by Plato and Aristotle, also had reason, or "the idea," as its basic

[44] § 29 below. All quotations in this paragraph are from § 29.

principle. It was also an idealistic philosophy. But reason, or thought, was not made all-comprehending. "Ancient philosophy left something existing apart from thought; it left a residue that was not absorbed in thought." This something was matter—the substratum of reality. Ancient philosophy knew well to guard the difference between thought and being, between reason and matter. This borderline was violated by neo-Platonism. The distinction of neo-Platonism was to go a step beyond ancient philosophy and incorporate matter into the "idea." Thereupon, there is nothing outside reason. Thought is the sole reality.

> Fatherland, family, worldly ties, and goods in general, which the ancient peripatetic philosophy still counted as man's bliss—all these are nothing for the neo-Platonic sage. He even considers death better than corporeal life; he does not include the body in his essence. . . .

Thus, Plotinus was ashamed to have a body.

But, where man has nothing apart from his thought, he searches for and finds everything in his thought. The concrete, sensuous, real world of matter is now included in thought. It is not denied completely; it is denied only an independent existence apart from thought. "Thought negates everything, but only in order to posit everything in itself." Matter is ideated and made an attribute of thought. "That which is the function and concern of the senses, of perception and of life, becomes the function and concern of thought." Ideal being is substituted in the absence of real being. The essence of the reality that the neo-Platonist lost is now attributed by him to his conceptions and ideas. "Precisely because he no longer relates himself as a subject to a real world as his object, his conceptions become for him objects, beings, spirits, and gods." And reason, because it no longer has a boundary outside itself, posits matter as its boundary, as its otherness, within itself. "So does reason, the idea, become concrete." But this concreteness is merely a predicate and a determination of thought, "for the proposition 'the notion is concrete' is identical with the proposition 'being is a determination of thought.'" Only thought that is absolutely limitless and all-inclusive is being and reality. The essence of neo-Platonism was the elimination of all limitation and distinction from true being. True and ultimate reality is "simple, singular, simply undetermined, and indistinct." Thus, it excludes even mind, notion, and being as the ultimate reality, for these, too, are still determined and not absolutely simple and all-comprehending. Thus, the ultimate reality, the God, of neo-Platonism is beyond all determination. "To have no longer any distinction, to have no mind or self, is and means being God."

Neo-Platonism, Feuerbach maintains, is no longer philosophy; it is truly theology. "The so-called neo-Platonic philosophy . . . differentiates itself from ancient philosophy only in that it is theology" (§ 58 below). The One of neo-Platonism is but the God of theology. The God of theology "is nothing but the essence of reason itself" (§ 6). Neo-Platonism is identified with theology precisely because its essential orientation is theological. It is the essence of theology to abstract from all that is sensuous, concrete, and material, placing the abstraction in God. The God of theology is the sole and ultimate reality. He is the infinite being, the being without any limitation and boundary, who is elevated above the limits of matter and sensation (§ 6). As such, he is an unconditioned, independent, and self-sufficient being "who needs no other being for his own being, consequently existing by and through himself" (§ 6). All reality is placed in God, and apart from him nothing is real. Matter in itself has no reality. It is real only to the extent that it is part of the divine, as God's creation. This, the unreality of matter in itself is the most fundamental consideration in Feuerbach's evaluation of the various philosophical and theological systems. It is the "Geiger counter" by which he discovers their true essence. All else will follow from it.

By the same token, using the independent reality of matter as the criterion, Feuerbach proceeds to identify the Hegelian system, not only with neo-Platonism, but now also with its equivalent, theology. Theology, neo-Platonism, and the Hegelian system are one and the same thing. Thus, "Hegel is not 'the German or Christian Aristotle'—he is the German Proclus. Absolute philosophy is the reborn Alexandrian philosophy" (§ 29). And "the secret of 'absolute' philosophy is thus the secret of theology" (§ 23). "The Hegelian philosophy is the last refuge, the last rational support, of theology" (§ 14). "The essence of speculative philosophy is nothing but the rationalized, realized, presented essence of God. Speculative philosophy is the true, consistent, and rational theology" (§ 5).

Hegel's theory of being reveals its true neo-Platonic and theological colors. Being in itself has no reality. It is simply the undetermined and unmediated object of thought (§ 27). It is a general notion without specificity or particularity (§ 27). Reality resides, not in being, but in thought. Thought is the beginning, the middle, and the end of reality. The circle is thus truly the symbol of the Hegelian philosophy. It is a self-enclosed circle of absolute thought (§ 48). Being in itself, or matter, is deprived of all reality. This is, according to Feuerbach, but the premise of neo-Platonism and theology.

Similarly, as in neo-Platonism and theology, the more we abstract from the concrete and material world, the more material and sensuous is our abstraction, so also with Hegel. Hegel's abstract thought culminates in "the concrete notion." Only "the concrete notion" is the true notion (§ 30). "The concrete notion" thus expresses the recognition of the truth of concreteness. But this concreteness is placed in the notion, that is, in thought. It is the idea of concreteness, the thought of the individual, that "the concrete notion" expresses, not the independent, real, and concrete individual. "Hegel is a realist . . . he is a realist in the abstraction from all reality" (§ 30). Even in tracing the process by which the notion becomes "the concrete notion," Hegel is only following the path taken by the "rationalized God of theology" in his process of actualization.

According to Hegel, the concrete notion, the idea, is at first only abstract and only in the element of thought; it is the rationalized

God of theology before the creation of the world. But, as God manifests, reveals, temporalizes, and actualizes himself, so does the idea realize itself; Hegel is the history of theology transformed into a logical process. (§ 31)

Essentially, Hegel's idealism is but the expression of theology and neo-Platonism in a conceptual, logical form. Hegel's philosophy

does not negate the dogmas of theology, but only restores and mediates them through the negation of rationalism. The secret of the Hegelian dialectic lies, in the last analysis, only in the fact that he negates theology by philosophy and then, in turn, negates philosophy by theology. Theology constitutes the beginning and the end. . . . At first everything is overthrown, but then everything is put again in its former place. . . . (§ 21)

This "former place" which is the beginning and the end of theology and speculative philosophy and which is the essential ground and foundation on which they stand is the monistic view of the ultimate unity of reality and thought. The unity of God in theology is the unity of thinking and that which is thought. This unity, Feuerbach declares, is but the secret of speculative thought. As in theology all things are in God, so in Hegel all things are in the absolute mind. Hegel's absolute mind is but the God of theology and neo-Platonism. This monistic view, which claims to have reconciled and united being and thought, matter and spirit, the finite and the infinite, received its most complete formulation in Hegel. This view, Feuerbach claims, is, however, nothing but the expression of rational mysticism.[45]

Feuerbach centers his attack against Hegel precisely on this point, that is, the monistic view that is based on the identity of being and thought. He thus directs his critique at the very foundation of Hegel's philosophy, based as it is on the claim that all contradictions have been reconciled in the absolute idea. Philosophy and theology, notion and existence, thought

[45] There are a number of modern scholars who agree with Feuerbach that there are mystical elements in Hegel. Richard Kroner would seem to be one; see *Von Kant bis Hegel* (Tübingen: J. C. B. Mohr, 1921), p. 272. See also Alfred Bäumler, *Hegels Geschichte der Philosophie*, p. 36.

and being—all these are now claimed by Hegel to have been reconciled in his philosophy. Feuerbach's critique undertakes to negate this dialectical identity and reconciliation of the Hegelian philosophy.[46] The basic reconciliation, in the Hegelian system from which all else will follow, is that of being and thought. "The identity of thought and being . . . is the central point of the philosophy of identity" (§ 24 below). Feuerbach is, therefore, dealing exclusively in his critique with the Hegelian claim to have reconciled being and thought. It is this that he undertakes to refute.

Feuerbach's main argument is that the reconciliation is not a true reconciliation that has succeeded in overcoming the differences between two distinct and independent entities—that is, thought and being—thus establishing their identity. It is not as Hegel claimed that he proceeded from the presuppositionless beginning of pure being, making his way toward the ultimate reconciliation in absolute mind. Absolute mind, the reconciliation, was the presupposition underlying his philosophy from the very start. "That the beginning is made with being is a mere formality, for it is not the true beginning, the true first; a beginning might just as well have been made with the absolute idea, for to Hegel himself, even before he wrote his *Logic,* that is, presented his logical ideas in a scientific form, the absolute idea was a certainty, an immediate truth." [47] The reconciliation was possible, Feuerbach argues, simply because there was never a true reconciliation to be made. Hegel starts with thought and ends with thought. He starts with absolute mind and ends with it. He never goes out of thought to deal with true, independent being. All reconciliation in Hegel's philosophy is reconciliation within thought, not the reconciliation of thought and being. The being that Hegel reconciles with thought is an ideated being from the beginning before reconciliation took place. The "otherness" of thought, the object, is in Hegel's philosophy

[46] Löwith, *Von Hegel zu Nietzsche,* p. 87.
[47] *Sämtliche Werke,* II, 209.

already within thought. Both thinking and its differentiation, the "otherness" of thinking, is within thought.

According to Hegel, philosophy has for an object only "that which is"; but this "is" is itself only an abstracted and ideated "is." Hegel is a thinker who surpasses himself in thought; he wants to grasp the thing itself, but in the thought of the thing. He wants to be apart from thought, but within thought itself. . . . (§ 30 below)

Thus, the being of which Hegel speaks is in truth only thought itself, but not real being; the Hegelian reconciliation has been of thought with itself, but not of thought and true being.

The Hegelian philosophy did not overcome the contradiction of thought and being. That being with which the *Phenomenology* starts stands in the most direct contradiction to real being no less than that being with which the *Logic* starts. (§ 28)

All that the Hegelian reconciliation has shown is the self-sufficiency of thought within its system. What Hegel is really saying is that thought alone is real.

The essence of thought is presupposed from the start as the absolute and only true being—the real or actual can be recognized only in an indirect way and only as the essential and necessary adjective of the notion. (§ 30)

It maintains that spirit, or thought, is grounded in itself and that, in order for anything else, like nature or man, to have being, it must be grounded in thought.[48] Hegel, in the true tradition of idealism, equates "I am" with "I think," making nature and the world merely the "alter ego," with the emphasis on the "ego."[49] Hegel's absolute identity was in truth absolute one-sidedness—the one-sidedness of thought and self-consciousness. The motto of the Hegelian philosophy, therefore, could well be: "That which is not thought of does not exist" (§ 35 below). The presupposition of Hegel's philosophy was the philosophical presupposition of self-consciousness, not the unphilosophical beginning of life. In a statement

48 Löwith, *Von Hegel zu Nietzsche,* p. 89.
49 *Ibid.,* p. 89.

that reminds one of Kierkegaard, Feuerbach describes Hegel as the example of a self-sufficient, professional thinker whose real existence was secured by the state and consequently remained without significance for his philosophy. As such, Hegel did not know real existence and real life. Only the isolated thinker who is removed from the real, concrete world could maintain the supremacy and self-sufficiency of abstract thought. "The absolute spirit is nothing but the absolute professor."[50]

Feuerbach rejects this one-sidedness of thought that is made the total and all-comprehending reality. "Thought that 'overleaps its otherness'—the 'otherness of thought' is, however, being—is thought that oversteps its natural boundaries" (§ 29 below). It claims for itself something that does not belong to it. This something is being. True and real being is irreducible to thought and must stand outside its domain. It cannot be incorporated into thought and still retain its truth and reality.

> This being is also—as it is drawn by speculative philosophy into its domain and claimed as its notion—a pure ghost, standing in absolute contradiction to real being and to that which man understands by being. (§ 26)

True being must remain being-for-itself, actual and objective. It cannot be a mere being-for-others, a predicate or an adjective of something else, namely, of thought. "Being in thought, without objectivity, reality, or being-for-itself, is, of course, nothing" (§ 26). For being to be true being, it must be something other than thought.

> The proof that something is has no other meaning than that something is not only thought of. This proof cannot, however, be derived from thought itself. If being is to be added to an object of thought, so must something distinct from thought be added to thought itself. (§ 25)

This something that is distinct from thought and that must be a property of being is particularity. Thought consists of

[50] *Ausgewählte Briefe,* II, 120.

general and universal concepts. The "this" of logic and thought applies universally to all instances. For thought, "this" and "universal" "flow together" and are "indistinguishable" (§ 28). But, in truth, "what an immense difference there is between the 'this' as an object of abstract thought and the 'this' as an object of reality!" (§ 28). Thought that consists of words and concepts cannot, therefore, grasp and represent the object in its true reality, that is, in its irreducible particularity. But Hegel's system was based precisely on the claim that this can be done, that the object in its true reality is grasped and represented in thought. Hegel's system was therefore based on an untenable contradiction, "the contradiction between the word, which is general, and the object, which is always a particular" (§ 28). By demonstrating this contradiction, Feuerbach argues, the entire system is refuted and must consequently be rejected.

V

Feuerbach's critique of Hegel is, thus, centered on the fundamental theme of the Hegelian philosophy, the reconciliation of being and thought. And the essence of Feuerbach's critique is that it was a sham reconciliation, the reconciliation of thought with itself and not with real being. These two aspects of Feuerbach's critique reflect a widespread trend in post-Hegelian philosophy. The Hegelian reconciliation is felt to be no longer satisfactory and, as such, comes to serve as the main target for criticism. Feuerbach's critique of Hegel, in its negative and destructive aspect, is by no means unique or even original. We find the same line of critique in Immanuel Hermann Fichte, Friedrich Julius Stahl, Heinreich Moritz Chalybäus, Friedrich Adolf Trendelenburg, Christopher H. Weisse, Kuno Philip Fischer and in the better-known names of Schelling (his later period), Kierkegaard, and Marx. They all criticize the Hegelian reconciliation on the ground that it did not represent, and therefore did not reconcile, true being and existence. Indeed, I. H. Fichte strongly attacked Feuerbach in his *Zeitschrift für Philosophie und spekulative Theologie*[1] for not giving credit to those who preceded him in formulating the critique of the Hegelian reconciliation. Thus, Feuerbach, to the extent that he negates the Hegelian reconciliation, is merely one voice in the large chorus that was raised against Hegel. The post-Hegelian period of the 1830's and 1840's can be succinctly described as the period of the dissolution of the Hegelian reconciliation.[2]

But, although the post-Hegelians were in agreement about their dissatisfaction and criticism of the Hegelian reconciliation, when it came to offering a positive substitute for and a solution to the crisis that emerged as a result of their rejection of the Hegelian reconciliation, they fell into violent disagreement, each offering his own solution. In order to appreciate Feuerbach's distinct position, we must clearly delineate the issues involved in the Hegelian reconciliation that gave rise to the division among the post-Hegelians. Hegel's reconciliation was based on two claims. First, reconciliation is to be achieved on the basis of the identity of pure, or speculative, thought and being; namely, the identity of thought and being is to be achieved in philosophical thought. Second, speculative thought has indeed achieved that stage in its development where being is in reality reconciled with speculative thought.[3]

[1] *Ausgewählte Briefe,* IV, 291–293.

[2] This point is strongly emphasized by Löwith in his *Von Hegel zu Nietzsche,* and by Rawidowicz, *Ludwig Feuerbachs Philosophie.*

[3] On this point, there is, however, some ambiguity in Hegel. It is best exemplified by the famous statement in *The Philosophy of Right* that "what is real is rational, and what is rational is real." There is a double meaning in "what is." Does Hegel mean what is now existing or the reality that, although it does not exist now, ought to exist? In the first instance he would seem to be the defender of the *status quo,* the arch-conservative, whereas in the second instance he can be interpreted as revolutionary, demanding change in order to actualize the real in existence. This ambiguity runs through much of Hegel's writings. (See Löwith, *Von Hegel zu Nietzsche,* pp. 185–186.) It would seem that the revolutionary, critical element was stronger in the Jena Hegel, whereas the conserva-

Thus, the estrangement of the world in all its manifestations has finally been mediated. Eternity and temporality, infinity and the finite, reason and reality, essence and existence, spirit and the material, the inner and the external, religion and the state, Christianity and pagan philosophy, the individual and society, the citizen and the private person, ethics and legality—all are declared to have been reconciled in the Hegelian system. These claims come under attack, however, in the post-Hegelian period. In this respect, Feuerbach's critique is similar to that of I. H. Fichte, Schelling, Kierkegaard, and Marx. The distinction emerges when we consider what these men had to offer in place of the Hegelian reconciliation.

I. H. Fichte and his group, the Fichte-Ulrici circle, are in essence closest to the Hegelian spirit. Their critique was directed against the way in which Hegel established the identity of thought and being. It was their aim to show that the Hegelian system, though continually postulating the identity of thought and being, never succeeds in proving this identity.[4] They did not deny, however, the necessity and need of the principle of identity for philosophy. On the contrary, they strongly maintained the philosophic need for the ideal of the identity of thought and being. Thus, I. H. Fichte writes that philosophy "as the science of truth in itself cannot allow giving up the fundamental idea of the unity of thought and being in its totality."[5] Feuerbach, on the other hand, totally rejects this principle of the identity of thought and being. It is not that Hegel did not succeed in satisfactorily proving it or that a better formulation may be found. The principle itself is

---

tive element came to dominate the later Hegel. (See Marcuse, *Reason and Revolution,* pp. 42, 92, 96.) The revolutionary element would link Hegel directly with the revolutionary, left-wing post-Hegelians, Marx in particular.

4 See, for example, C. H. Weisse, *Über das Verhältniss des Publicums zur Philosophie der Zeitpunkte von Hegel's Abscheiden* (Leipzig, 1832), pp. 27–32.

5 *Zeitschrift für Philosophie und spekulative Theologie,* XIII (1844), 310.

untenable and is, indeed, the cause of all the harm that was created by the philosophy of idealism and by theology.[6]

The attempt, therefore, by Schelling and his followers—anti-Hegelians such as Hubert Beckers, J. H. Pabst, Leopold Schmid, and Anthon Günther—to substitute an intuitive "positive" philosophy for Hegel's absolute philosophy is rejected by Feuerbach with equal vehemence. Schelling, too, does not get away from the principle of identity. His critique of Hegel is directed, not against the principle, but against the Hegelian claim to have realized the principle in speculative-philosophical reason. This, Schelling claims, is untenable.[7] His critique is essentially the same as that outlined above; namely, he maintains the impossibility of arriving at true, real being from the activity of pure, speculative reason. All that one gets through the activity of speculative reason is ideated being. To this extent, Feuerbach is close to Schelling and is, no doubt, indebted to him. Schelling cannot, however, free himself from his idealistic moorings. He thus continues to hold fast to the principle of identity and claims anew its realization. He merely shifts the ground on which the principle is to be established. True, it cannot be established in speculative reason, but it can be established, Schelling now claims, in the imagination through an esthetic-intellectual intuition.

Feuerbach is vehemently and viciously critical of this position.[8] Of course, because Schelling does not establish the principle of identity in speculative thought, Feuerbach's criticism of Schelling cannot be the same as his criticism, which, indeed,

[6] For Feuerbach, as was pointed out before, the philosophy of idealism and theology are essentially the same, precisely because both are based on the principle of identity.

[7] This critique appears as early as 1834 in a preface to a work by Cousin and in his Munich lectures on the history of modern philosophy. See *Sämtliche Werke,* I, 126 ff. and 212 ff.

[8] Feuerbach's critique of Schelling's philosophical position is continuously interspersed with derogatory personal accusations and characterizations.

Schelling himself shared, of Hegel's principle of identity—the criticism that real being can never be grasped and represented in speculative thought, thus excluding the possibility of a true and valid identity between the two. Feuerbach's critique of Schelling is, therefore, directed against what Feuerbach claims is the total and arbitrary obscurantism of Schelling's "positive" philosophy. Feuerbach's critique cannot be philosophically formulated because, in his eyes, Schelling's philosophy has given up all philosophical criteria and standards, rejecting the criterion of truth, the necessity of thinking and the difference between reason and absurdity.[9] One cannot philosophically argue with and criticize such a system. One can only point out its true nature and then proceed to ignore it. This is precisely what Feuerbach does. For him, Schelling's "positive" philosophy is the worst kind of obscure mysticism and theosophy. It is "the fall of philosophy," [10] a "groundless, childish fantasy," [11] "the old philosophy with the conceit, the illusion of being the new *Realphilosophie*." [12] "One need only open his lectures to fall unconscious before the corpselike odor of Scotist scholasticism and Jakob Böhme's theosophy." [13] It is nonsense in the highest sense, mere stupidity.[14] And, having castigated Schelling's philosophy in no uncertain terms, Feuerbach proceeds to ignore him.

Thus, Feuerbach clearly establishes his distinction from his fellow critics of the Hegelian principle of identity. His positive position clearly differs from that of the Fichte-Ulrici cir-

[9] See Feuerbach's long letter to Marx answering the latter's invitation to write a comprehensive critique of Schelling in the *Deutsch-französische Jahrbücher; Ausgewählte Briefe,* II, 127 ff.

[10] *Sämtliche Werke,* VI, 280.

[11] *Ibid.,* 301; as quoted in S. Rawidowicz, *Ludwig Feuerbachs Philosophie,* p. 280.

[12] *Ibid.,* II, 260; as quoted in S. Rawidowicz, p. 280.

[13] *Ausgewählte Briefe,* II, 128.

[14] For further characterizations in this vein of Schelling's philosophy, see *Sämtliche Werke,* VII, 131–139, 258, 310, 390.

cle, which wanted merely to correct and improve the methodology of Hegel, and that of the Schelling-Baader circle, which wanted to re-establish the identity in the esthetic-intuitive imagination. Against both, Feuerbach maintains a dualistic position rejecting the monistic principle of identity, thus safeguarding an independent reality for being. For Feuerbach, real and true being is always particular, thus resisting all attempts at generalization and systematization that threaten to "swallow up" the particular in its individuality.

Feuerbach's defense of the particularity of being reminds one of Kierkegaard and his critique of the Hegelian system.[15] Kierkegaard also maintains that true being is always particular and individual. Thus, his central category is that of "the single one" in which alone truth and reality reside. Kierkegaard's attack on the Hegelian system is directed toward its "world process" in the defense of the "single one" in order to safeguard, like Feuerbach, the reality of the particular and individual being.[16] For the sake of "the single one," the Hegelian reconciliation achieved through the mediation and unity of reason and reality is rejected, and the split between essence and existence, God and the world, the inner and the external, religion and the state is reasserted.[17]

An even more striking similarity is seen in the fact that both Feuerbach and Kierkegaard center their attention on the problem of religion or, more specifically, of Christianity. The Hegelian reconciliation is understood primarily as it affects Christianity, that is, the reconciliation of God and the world or the spiritual and the material or the infinite and the finite. And, similarly, the rejection of the Hegelian reconciliation is undertaken for the sake of safeguarding the true essence of Christianity. Feuerbach, no less than Kierkegaard, claims to

[15] Feuerbach, of course, did not know Kierkegaard's writings and consequently did not formulate his position against him as he did against Schelling. Our comparison cannot, therefore, draw on Feuerbach's own understanding of his relation to Kierkegaard.

[16] Löwith, *Von Hegel zu Nietzsche,* p. 126.

[17] *Ibid.,* p. 58.

speak in the name of true, authentic Christianity and merely to explicate its hidden essence.[18]

But precisely at this point, where the similarity is so striking, the huge gap that divides Feuerbach from Kierkegaard develops in their understanding of the true essence of Christianity. For Feuerbach, the true, although hidden, essence of Christianity is man. True Christianity is anthropology. Christian theology "long ago became anthropology." [19] Its true concern, as expressed by Luther, is no longer with God in himself, but with the God "who is for me." Though it continues to speak in terms of God and the supernatural, its subject is really man and the natural world. Feuerbach reduces the split between God and the world, the infinite and the finite, the spiritual and the material, the transcendent and the immanent, the inner and the external, the supernatural and the natural into the exclusively worldly, finite, material, immanent, external, and natural.

Kierkegaard, *per contra,* understands Christianity exclusively in terms of the spiritual, transcendental God. Christianity is not a part of the natural and human world. It belongs to the spiritual realm of eternity. And to be a Christian means for Kierkegaard to transcend the temporality of the world and stand before God as "the single one" without the world. Kierkegaard, too, reduces the split, but in the direction opposite to that of Feuerbach. Christianity lives in God, in the spiritual, in the infinite, in the transcendent, and in the supernatural. Hegel, whose fundamental sin was to unite and mediate, presents his philosophy as the intellectual interpretation of Christianity whose very essence was the mediation and union of God and man in Jesus Christ. For Hegel, the very truth of Christianity lay in the fact that the Christ brought the mediation of the divine and the human. The Christian message for him is that man becomes God. "The Kingdom of God" is but the mediation of the earthly and the divine in "the

18 *Essence of Christianity,* pp. 42–43. See also Barth, *Die Theologie und die Kirche,* pp. 214–217.

19 *Essence of Christianity,* p. 38.

intellectual kingdom."[20] This Hegelian understanding of Christianity as "the intellectual kingdom" that mediates and unites the divine and the human is rejected by both Feuerbach and Kierkegaard. Feuerbach rejects it in favor of an exclusively "human kingdom," whereas Kierkegaard rejects it in the name of an exclusively "divine kingdom." This is clearly illustrated in the respective attitudes of Feuerbach and Kierkegaard to the implications of science, politics, and social developments in the modern world. Both recognize that these represent a contradiction to supernatural religion and that a break exists between the two. Having rejected the Hegelian attempt of mediation, an either/or situation confronts both Feuerbach and Kierkegaard. Feuerbach rejects supernatural religion, arguing that in fact and in practice people have already rejected it. What remains to be done is to overthrow it theoretically, which he proceeds to undertake to do.[21] Kierkegaard, on the other hand, rejects science and modern society as irrelevant to the religious life in which reality resides.[22]

The difference between Feuerbach and Kierkegaard in their respective interpretations of Christianity reflects also the difference between their respective conceptions of what constitutes "the essence of man." For Feuerbach, it is the concrete, flesh-and-blood, corporeal man. For Kierkegaard, it is the spirit of man that knows eternity.[23] Thus, Christianity for Feuerbach, when properly explicated, is an anthropology dealing with the needs, wants, and desires of sensuous, concrete man. For Kierkegaard, it is a matter of eternal, spiritual truth which transcends the temporality of sensuous man and his society. For each, religion addresses the essence and reality of man as each conceives them.

What underlies, however, the divergence between Feuer-

[20] Löwith, *Von Hegel zu Nietzsche,* pp. 60–61.

[21] *Sämtliche Werke,* VII, 32.

[22] *Either/Or,* trans. David F. and Lillian M. Swenson (Princeton: Princeton University Press, 1944), pp. 123 ff.

[23] *Attack upon Christendom,* trans. Walter Lowrie (Princeton: Princeton University Press, 1944).

bach and Kierkegaard is an even more fundamental difference in their respective notions of what constitutes the proper criterion and standard of the reality of being. This question forms the very basis on which we can understand the complicated similarities and diversities that marked the post-Hegelians, both in their relation to Hegel and in their relation to one another. Hegel claims, as we have seen, that the reality of being and its criterion is given in speculative, philosophical thought; on this basis, Hegel offers his synthesis and reconciliation. Hegel's reconciliation collapses in the post-Hegelian period because his criterion of speculative, pure thought is rejected. The criticism of the post-Hegelians is directed mainly against Hegel's criterion, not his reconciliation. The reconciliation is rejected only as the consequence of their rejection of the criterion. The post-Hegelians were by and large united in their criticism of the Hegelian criterion. But, having rejected the Hegelian criterion of speculative, pure thought, the post-Hegelians must offer their own criterion, and here wide divergencies emerge. We have already dealt with the divergency between Schelling and Feuerbach. A similarly wide one divides Kierkegaard and Feuerbach.

Kierkegaard's criterion of being is limited to the being of the human subject. His concern is with the criterion for the authentic being that each individual person may realize. Kierkegaard's concern is thus centered on the being of the individual human person and not on the wider ontological question of being in general. His concern is "the single one." In this sense, his criterion for true being is internal and subjective. The truth and reality of being lie in the inner subjectivity and consciousness of "the single one." The criterion that Kierkegaard offers is the ethical-religious dimension of our consciousness. It is in the ethical and religious domain that "the single one" grasps or, better, realizes his authentic and true being. In experiencing himself as an ethical and religious person, "the single one" realizes his true being.

For Feuerbach, the criterion of true and real being is sense perception. Only in sense perception is being given as it really is without distortions or abstraction. The mark of true being is its particularity and independent existence. True being is always the particular "this" that occupies a specifically determined place in space and time. It is not contingent on our conscience for its being. Its being is out there, confronting us and given to us. Our consciousness can only receive it, not create or possess it. Sense perception becomes the sole measure of true and real being. Thus, whereas for Kierkegaard the truth and reality of being lie in the subject and are private and internal, for Feuerbach they lie in the object and are public and external. Whereas for Kierkegaard they are a task to be realized, for Feuerbach they are data to be received.

It is on the basis of this point—that is, Feuerbach's advocacy of sense perception as the criterion of the truth and reality of being—that his relation to Marx can also be understood. The relation between Feuerbach and Marx is seen by many scholars as a continuous line of development. Feuerbach starts the rebellion against the spiritualization and abstraction of the Hegelian system and in its place launches the concretization of man. Or, to put it in different language, Feuerbach starts the rebellion against the theology of Hegel and launches its reduction to anthropology. But he fails to carry his program to the end. His concept of man is, in the last analysis, not fully concretized, and his reduction of theology is not carried to its final conclusion. Indeed, although Feuerbach reduces theology to anthropology, he at the same time, so it is argued, elevates his anthropology into a theology.[24]

Marx, according to these interpretations, pushes the Feuerbachian program to its final conclusion. He is, so to speak, the consistent and thoroughgoing Feuerbachian who radically concretizes man and completely reduces theology. Thus, for example, even though Feuerbach rejects the subject of religion, that is, God, he stops short of rejecting also the predicate of religion, that is, the divine.[25] For Feuerbach, there is still something essentially human expressed in religion that he

[24] Löwith, *Von Hegel zu Nietzsche,* p. 362.
[25] *Ibid.,* p. 363.

wanted to preserve.[26] All he wants, therefore, is merely to show the earthly origins of religion. The divine attributes of religion are valid for man. They are only expressed in an upside-down fashion in theology, which can, after all, be corrected by inversion. This position is for Marx still "religious." It is a stopping in midstream. For Marx, Feuerbach's reduction of theology to anthropology is only the presupposition and beginning for the critique of human relations that is, after all, the paramount task.[27] Marx, therefore, goes beyond Feuerbach and raises the questions: "Why should the earthly transcend itself to heaven?"; "Why should theology and religion have arisen at all?" Though Feuerbach's critique stops with the demand for the humanization of God, Marx's critique demands the removal of the conditions that gave rise to the God of religion in the first place.[28] And, these conditions being in Marx's view social conditions, the critique of religion and theology is transformed into the critique of politics and economics. Thus, Marx, building on Feuerbach, pushes beyond him.

The same interpretation is given with regard to the concretization of man. Feuerbach is indeed moving toward the concretization of man in his critique of the Hegelian conception of man. In seeing the essence of man as spirit or reason, Hegel's conception is abstracted from the concrete, real man. Feuerbach's demand for the man of flesh and blood, of stomach and heart, is therefore an important and necessary step toward the concretization of man. But Feuerbach again did not go all the way. He stopped midway with what is still the bourgeois conception of man, namely, the private individual.[29] This is, for Marx, still an abstraction from the fully concretized man. The truly concretized man must be placed in a social context. His essence must not be severed from his

26 *Ibid.*, p. 377.
27 *Ibid.*, pp. 375–376.
28 *Ibid.*, p. 378.
29 *Ibid.*, p. 338.

social matrix or, for that matter, from his political powers. Here, again, Marx accepts Feuerbach's concretization of man with stomach and heart, but goes beyond him to place this man in the political and economic context of his society.

There is no denying that these interpretations represent a true side of the relation between Feuerbach and Marx. Evidently, Feuerbach had an impact on Marx. As Engels once wrote, "We all became at once Feuerbachians." [30] Feuerbach appeared as the great liberator, the demolisher of speculative theologies and abstract philosophical systems. Marx is, no doubt, indebted to Feuerbach for this liberation, and he acknowledges this when he writes: "There is no other road to truth and freedom . . . than the road through the 'brook of fire' (Feuer-bach). Feuerbach is the purgatory of our time." [31]

But to see Feuerbach's relation to Marx exclusively in this light is to overlook the substantive and basic difference between the two. The cause of this separation is again Feuerbach's turning to sense perception as the criterion and basis of his philosophy. Here Marx is worlds apart from Feuerbach. Feuerbach's anthropology of sense perception could not lead to Marx's activist and revolutionary social thought. Nor could it lead to Marx's view of man as primarily placed in the historical, social, and economic context. It is not that Feuerbach went part of the way and Marx merely continued on the same way by drawing more consistently and radically the implications that Feuerbach's position contained all along. Feuerbach's basic commitment to sense perception would prevent him from following the path of Marx. It committed him to a view diametrically opposed to that of Marx, one that maintained that the truth and reality of being reside in the object, in nature, and are independent of the activity of the human subject. The human subject must be placed in nature as a passive ego. There is no continuous line of development from

30 K. Marx and F. Engels, *Selected Works,* II (Moscow: Foreign Language Publication House, 1951), 333.

31 Marx-Engels, *Historisch-kritische Gesamtausgabe,* I, 1, p. 175.

this to Marx's view that places man in the historical context as an active and revolutionary agent who can determine the social, political, and economic conditions of his life. Indeed, on this fundamental point, Marx is more truly an heir of Hegel, particularly the Jena Hegel, than of Feuerbach. Consequently, Marx sides with Hegel and against Feuerbach on three basic issues. First, on the question of sense certainty. Sense certainty for Marx, as indeed also for Hegel, is not the final and ultimate criterion of truth.[32] Second, he follows Hegel in the dialectical method. He reproaches Feuerbach for his lack of dialectic and holds him responsible for the opinion prevalent in Germany at the time that Hegel's dialectic was "a dead horse." Feuerbach, he writes to Engels, "has much to answer for in this respect." [33] And, third, he attaches his thought to Hegel's analysis of the processes of labor, which he views as being of the utmost significance.[34] Feuerbach does not deal with this question at all.

Once the dazzle of Feuerbach's critique of Hegel passed away, the basic differences that separate him from Marx became clear. Marx now turns from admiration to severe criticism,[35] passing the judgment that, "compared to Hegel, Feuerbach is very poor." [36] Once the thought of Feuerbach could be seen in its totality with all its implications, Feuerbach could only be an object of criticism or disinterest for Marx. Feuerbach performed his significant part for Marx in his negative critique of Hegel, valid insofar as it negated the abstract, theological, idealistic, and spiritual form of Hegel's philosophy, offering a realistic anthropological form in its

32 See Marcuse, *Reason and Revolution,* p. 271.

33 Marx and Engels, *Selected Correspondence (1846–1895),* trans. and ed. Dona Torr, Marxist Library, XXIX (New York: The International Publishers, 1935), 233.

34 See the marked influence of the chapter "Master and Bondsman" in *The Phenomenology of Mind* on Marx's analysis of the labor process in his *Historisch-kritische Gesamtausgabe,* III, 86, 89–90 ff.

35 See Marx, *Theses on Feuerbach.*

36 Marx, *Selected Correspondence,* XXIX, 169. See also Löwith, *Von Hegel zu Nietzsche,* pp. 334, 431.

place. Insofar as Feuerbach destroys the Hegelian system and humanizes the God of theology, he is moving in the right direction. To the extent that Feuerbach rejects the Hegelian claim that reconciliation is an accomplished fact, his position is laudable. In short, Feuerbach is important for Marx in being a "liberator" and a "purgatory."

But, when Feuerbach comes to offer the positive formulation of his own philosophy of sense certainty, he is worlds apart from Marx. Marx's thought is an instance of what Marcuse calls negative thinking.[37] The truth is not found in the given objects; it is to be realized by man's rational activity. And, in the process of realization, the given objects are negated and destroyed so as to enable the realization of man's true essence and potentialities. Thus, the realization of the truth requires man to undertake revolutionary and destructive action against the given objects. The demand is put forth to change the given reality so that it may conform to reason.[38] Feuerbach's philosophy of sense certainty is, on the other hand, an instance of what Marcuse calls positivism.[39] Truth is given in the object that confronts us, and the ultimate method of its verification lies in the observation of the object. Here, the realization of truth requires a change in man's consciousness so that it may conform to the given objects. The negation and transformation are to take place in man's consciousness and not in the given objects. Truth is realized when man's reason is brought into conformity with the given reality.

Thus, in viewing Feuerbach's philosophy in the context of post-Hegelian philosophy, we must maintain a balanced judgment. We must acknowledge the points of contact and similarity that Feuerbach has with the other post-Hegelians in the critique of the Hegelian reconciliation, but we must also see the distinct character of his philosophy of sense certainty.

[37] *Reason and Revolution,* p. vii.

[38] Löwith, *Von Hegel zu Nietzsche,* p. 113.

[39] *Reason and Revolution,* p. 27.

VI

The *Principles* was first published in Zürich in 1843.[1] Feuerbach entertained great hopes for the *Principles.* He considered the work to have expressed most forcefully and comprehensively his total position and thus to be the culmination, not only of his *Thesen zur Reform der Philosophie,* but also of *The Essence of Christianity.* He expected the *Principles* to establish his position beyond question and to exercise a strong impact on the history of theology and religion. As he says in the preface: "The consequences of these principles will certainly follow." But they did not follow, at least not immediately. Most of his contemporaries reacted negatively or, at best, in a lukewarm fashion to the work.[2] As for future generations, the work sank into oblivion (with, of course, certain exceptions). It certainly never achieved the impact or prominence of *The Essence of Christianity.* And yet it seems that Feuerbach was right in considering the *Principles* the summation and culmination of his work. Is it possible to account for this discrepancy? Can its "failure" be explained? The cause seems to lie in the fact that the *Principles* is constructed in a way that is not immediately clear.

Although it is a fairly short work, it is, nevertheless, highly complicated. A wealth of material is thrown at the reader in what appears to be a highly disorganized manner. The work is polemical, argumentative, and critical. It abounds in historical material and illustrations that, although they offer suggestive insights into and evaluations of the history of modern philosophy, nevertheless seem to have little bearing on the main thesis. The reader is simply lost in a maze of involved

[1] The English translation offered here is of the text that appeared in the collected works of Feuerbach edited by Wilhelm Bolin and Friedrich Jodl (Stuttgart: Frommanns Verlag, 1904).

[2] See Rawidowicz, *Ludwig Feuerbachs Philosophie,* pp. 152–156, for a résumé of the various reactions to the *Principles* among Feuerbach's contemporaries.

argumentation. He seems to be given at random a mass of interesting and suggestive thoughts on a great variety of subjects which, however, lead nowhere in particular. This lack of organization is the main weakness of the work.

It is all the more strange that the question of structure should be so bothersome here, for the very title of the work denotes a positive and straightforward declaration of basic principles. The *Principles* is offered as the manifesto of Feuerbach's "new philosophy," and nothing should be more straightforward than the structure of a manifesto. Quite clearly, the *Principles,* although offered as a manifesto, is not structured as such. Can we account for the discrepancy?

Feuerbach tells us in the preface that his original intention was to offer a detailed and voluminous work. For some reason (he blames it on the German censor), he changed his mind, cut the manuscript "like a barbarian," and offered the result as a declaration of principles. But he did not change the structure of the work to correspond to its new, abbreviated form. The structure remained that of a detailed and voluminous work, not a declaration of principles. This alone would have doubtless contributed to the awkwardness and ambiguity of the work's effect. It is difficult to condense the substance of a voluminous work into an outline and yet keep the clarity of the over-all structure. Unfortunately, the outline was not particularly successful. The "cutting," it seems, was not skillful. Certain points that require greater elaboration were left epigrammatic and ambiguous, whereas other points that are quite obvious were repeated again and again. Thus, although the structure of the *Principles* is not clear and evident,[3] it is there, nevertheless, and in the following pages an attempt to delineate it will be made.

[3] Another difficulty that should be mentioned in this connection is due to a characteristic of Feuerbach's style. Feuerbach often first presents the reader with the conclusion stated succinctly and in sweeping generalities. He then proceeds to argue and substantiate his conclusion. This is often involved and dry argumentation. At times, the conclusion is repeated at the end of the argument, and at times it is not.

In his preface to the *Principles,* which he edited anew in 1922, Hans Ehrenberg divides the work into three parts: (1) §§ 1–16, which contain the critique of pre-Kantian philosophy; (2) §§ 17–31, which contain the polemic against post-Kantian philosophy; and (3) §§ 32–65, which are the positive presentation of the "new philosophy." Although there seems to be general agreement about §§ 32–65 as the positive presentation of the new philosophy, the difficulty arises in the evaluation of §§ 1–31. Ehrenberg evidently considers them as merely a historical review and therefore divides them on a purely chronological basis. Even if Ehrenberg's chronological division did correspond strictly to the actual division of the work (it does not),[4] it would still not have presented the essential intent of these sections. True, §§ 1–31 contain a great deal of historical material. But they are not intended purely as a historical review presented in chronological order. Their intent is the analysis of certain theological and philosophical formulations. History is used as the background to provide the illustrations; after all, these formulations did express themselves in certain historical instances. But the historical-chronological dimension of the work affords merely the matrix in which the thematic material is elaborated and exemplified. Sections 1–32 must, therefore, be understood thematically with thematic subdivisions. Feuerbach has a point to make, and the structure of the work must be understood with reference to this point. A mere chronological division misses the intent and import of the work.

If the *Principles* consisted of §§ 24–58, there would have been no problem with its structure. Feuerbach is dealing here with two basic and mutually exclusive philosophic viewpoints. On the one hand is the Hegelian speculative system built on the principle of abstract and absolute mind. On the other hand is what Feuerbach calls "the new philosophy," which is built on the principle of sensation and feeling. Feuerbach's thesis is crystal-clear. He wants to negate the Hegelian speculative system and establish the "new philosophy" as the true

4 See Rawidowicz, *Ludwig Feuerbachs Philosophie,* p. 129.

and authentic philosophic formulation of reality as "it really is."

Thus, §§ 24–58 divide themselves structurally very neatly. Sections 24–31 constitute the criticism and negation of Hegelian speculative philosophy. The essence of the Hegelian system is seen to lie in the principle of the identity of thought and being, namely, that thought is the sum of truth and reality. Only that that can be thought is true and real. The substance of the critique revolves around one central point, namely, that the Hegelian system, by placing reality in thought, fails to account for and do justice to the concrete, individual, and particular being where, it is maintained, true reality resides. (For elaboration, see Part IV of this Introduction.) Sections 32–58 constitute the positive presentation of "the new philosophy." [5] Essentially, "the new philosophy" is vindicated precisely at the point that proved the negation of the Hegelian system; namely, the "new philosophy" can grasp without distortion and do justice to the particularity of the concrete, individual being. It can do so because it is based, not on pure, abstract thought, but on sense-perception. (For elaboration, see Part I of this Introduction.)

It is the remaining two parts, §§ 1–23 and 59–65, that are problematic regarding their structure and intent. If any attempt to grasp their significance is to succeed, however, they must be approached in terms of Feuerbach's central thesis in §§ 24–58, namely, the negation of the Hegelian system and the defense of "the new philosophy."

Sections 1–23 constitute the most difficult and complicated

[5] It is true that §§ 32–58 do contain much that is negative and polemical against speculative philosophy. This is due, however, to Feuerbach's temperament. He could not free himself from his polemical disposition. He was and remained the archrebel, the philosopher who criticizes and negates, rather than the constructive systematizer. Thus, even when he wants to construct, he can proceed only through polemics and criticism. This would account for the polemics in §§ 32–58. Their intent and main purpose, however, are beyond any question positive and constructive.

part of the work. To say that they are merely a historical review of pre-Hegelian philosophy is to dispose of the matter too easily. To wish that they were never included is a great temptation, but it seems evident that their exclusion would have greatly impoverished the work as a whole. They are far from being superfluous or merely a historical survey. One thing is, however, true; they are poorly constructed and are therefore likely to leave the reader more bewildered and confused than enlightened. This is owing primarily to two reasons. First, Feuerbach is trying to establish a great deal in a short space; second, he does not delineate clearly the various points he is making. Our task here, therefore, will be to attempt to distinguish the various substantive points that Feuerbach advances in these sections.

(1) Feuerbach, by broadening the historical perspectives of the work, is setting the polemic between the Hegelian speculative philosophy and "the new philosophy" in the widest possible context. The polemic is no longer merely a critique of Hegel's philosophy as such and an argument for yet another particular philosophy called "the new philosophy." The polemic is between two fundamental and all-comprehending *Weltanschauungen*. Feuerbach designates them as the theological and anthropological *Weltanschauungen*.

Anthropology is the *Weltanschauung* that takes matter as a real and independent being and therefore bases itself on sensation as the primary means of the authentic cognition of reality. We can know reality through the senses. The "truth of reality"—to use an expression of Feuerbach that is indeed a Hegelian heritage—is sensation. The anthropological view, however, does not exclude thought. On the contrary, it embraces thought, but thought based on sensation, thought guided and rectified by the senses and the material object that exists apart from us. The anthropological view is not the contradiction of thought as such, but of pure or abstract thought. Theology, on the other hand, is the *Weltanschauung* based on pure and abstract thought. Thought in itself and for itself is the sum of truth and reality. Only that which is a predicate or an object [6] of thought has truth and reality. Thought is the substance of reality, and only abstract, pure thought is the means to grasp and comprehend the truth of reality. It is thought that is divorced from sensation and matter.

These are two fundamental and eternally existing ways of comprehending the world and reality. In view of this, the traditional distinction between the religious and philosophic formulations of the world is set aside. The criterion now is the distinction between the theological and anthropological *Weltanschauungen*. Absolute mind and sensation now provide the two focal points by which classification is determined. On this basis, a new grouping is formed that includes both what would ordinarily be considered religious-theological, for example, theism and pantheism, and what would be considered philosophical, for example, the various forms of idealism. Here they are all grouped together as belonging to the theological *Weltanschauung,* for they all share the central orientation of the theological *Weltanschauung* in which abstract and absolute mind is ultimate reality.[7]

(2) Feuerbach undertakes the examination of the various expressions and formulations of the theological *Weltanschauung*. His purpose is to show how the theological *Weltanschauung* developed itself in the course of history toward an ever-growing self-consistency, culminating in Hegelian absolute idealism as the epitome of the theological *Weltanschauung*. He sketches brilliantly and with penetrating insight

[6] Feuerbach often uses the term "object" as equivalent to "predicate," that is, as a dependent being, a being for others. This is always the case when he contrasts "object" to "subject." "Subject" in these instances signifies an independent being, a being in itself.

[7] The fundamental step that joins theism and pantheism with the speculative philosophy of idealism is the identification of the concept of God with abstract and absolute mind. It is the basic neo-Platonic identity of the theological-religious formulation with the formulation of idealist metaphysics (§ 29). Feuerbach re-establishes this identity of God and absolute mind. The essence of reason or absolute mind is, he argues, precisely the essence of the God of theology.

the inner dynamics of the theological *Weltanschauung* as it moves through its various expressions—theism, pantheism, and the various formulations of idealism from Descartes and Leibniz through Kant and Fichte to Hegel—to an evermore-consistent and all-encompassing (in terms of the theological *Weltanschauung*) formulation. Idealism is shown to be the culmination of pantheism, which in turn is the culmination of theism. And, in idealism itself, Hegel is shown to be the culmination of Kant and Fichte, who in turn are the culmination of Descartes and Leibniz (§§ 7, 8, 10, 12, 15, 17, 21, 23). Feuerbach is preparing here the grounds for his criticism of the Hegelian system in §§ 24–31. The analysis of the various formulations shows that the Hegelian system is the highest and most consistent expression of the theological *Weltanschauung*. When Feuerbach, therefore, proceeds to criticize and negate the Hegelian system, he is negating the theological *Weltanschauung* in its culminating, consistent, and all-encompassing expression.

(3) Feuerbach has yet another purpose in reviewing the various formulations of the theological *Weltanschauung*. He introduces the thesis that the modern era—although itself theological—attempted to dissolve theology into anthropology, but in the last analysis failed because the dissolution was only a partial dissolution and was, indeed, itself theological. This is, strictly speaking, a historical thesis. It is an evaluation of modern thought. But the thesis is not introduced as an instance of historical scholarship for its own sake. Feuerbach has an ax to grind, namely, the establishment of "the new philosophy," and everything he does is related to this primary task. Thus, the thesis is introduced in order to place "the new philosophy" in the historical context. Modern philosophy tried and failed. "The new philosophy" and only "the new philosophy" can succeed. "The new philosophy" is not, therefore, proposing anything new. It is only the culmination of preceding philosophy. Thus, there is a tension and ambiguity in Feuerbach's position. On the one hand, "the new philosophy," as the complete expression of the anthropological *Welt-*

anschauung, is the direct antithesis of modern philosophy, which is the expression of the theological *Weltanschauung.* We have an either/or situation in which the realization of "the new philosophy" is the rejection of modern philosophy. On the other hand, "the new philosophy" is the continuation and culmination of modern philosophy. It realizes modern philosophy. In this respect, Feuerbach is a good Hegelian. Realization means negation. Feuerbach is in effect claiming for "the new philosophy" what Hegel claimed for his system of absolute idealism.

(4) To be able to follow Feuerbach's thesis and arguments, however, involves keeping in mind a duality of meaning—and therefore also an ambiguity of meaning—that he introduces into the terms "theology" and "anthropology." For, in addition to the formulation explicated above, Feuerbach introduces another: theology is a God-centered, whereas anthropology is a man-centered, *Weltanschauung.* Thus, in § 1, where Feuerbach formulates his thesis, he immediately presents the two aspects. "The task of the modern era was the realization and humanization of God—the transformation and dissolution of theology into anthropology." The dissolution of theology into anthropology is equivalent to the humanization of God. This formulation by and large runs parallel to the one given previously. The point of contact between the two formulations is established by identifying God with absolute reason (§ 6) and man with sensation and feeling (§ 36). Thus, the fundamental distinction between absolute, pure mind and sensation is maintained in the terms "God" and "man."

However, an additional aspect is introduced when the theological *Weltanschauung* is formulated in terms of God. This additional aspect which the term "God," so to speak, carries along with it can be called the theistic-religious aspect. God is a being separate and independent from man and the world. For "God . . . is God only when he is . . . distinguished from . . . man and nature" (§ 14). God is only God-in-himself. Thus, Feuerbach's identification of God with absolute reason is established specifically on the understanding of God as distinguished from man and nature. It is "God as God" who is "a nonhuman, nonsensuous being" that is identified with "the essence of reason itself" (§ 6). As a consequence, the term "theological" refers, not only to a *Weltanschauung* whose center is absolute mind, but also to a *Weltanschauung* in which God is a being independent of man and nature, a being-in-itself. The presence of either of these two meanings suffices in order for Feuerbach to characterize a formulation as "theological." The dissolution of the theological point of view will, therefore, be complete only when both aspects are dissolved. As long as one aspect remains—be it the aspect in which God is viewed as being independent of man or be it the aspect in which abstract thought is the primary principle—the formulation is condemned as "theological."

On this basis, Feuerbach puts forth his thesis that modern thought has failed in its attempt to dissolve theology because its dissolution was itself theological. It was "the negation of theology on the grounds of theology" [8] (§ 15). Each formulation of the theological *Weltanschauung*, while negating one aspect of the theological viewpoint, asserted the other aspect and so remained within the theological viewpoint. Namely, if it negated absolute mind as the primary principle, it nevertheless asserted the objective, independent existence of God; and, conversely, if it negated the objective, independent existence of God, it nevertheless asserted absolute mind as the primary principle. In either case, it was the negation of theology (as regards one aspect) on the grounds of theology (as regards the other aspect).

Feuerbach surveys the various formulations of the theological *Weltanschauung*, therefore, not only to trace its development toward a culmination in the Hegelian system, but also

[8] This statement should now be clear if it is remembered that the term "theology" has a twofold meaning inasmuch as it can refer to one or the other aspect of the theological viewpoint. In this statement, the term "theology" appears twice, but the points of reference are not identical. Once it refers to one aspect, whereas the second time it refers to the other aspect.

in order to demonstrate his thesis that the theological *Weltanschauung* (representing the modern era) negated itself, although it was a half-hearted negation which, in the last analysis, remained theological after all. In each expression of the theological *Weltanschauung*—theism, pantheism, and the various formulations of idealism—there is a negation of the theological viewpoint in one of its meanings but always coupled with an affirmation of its other meaning (§§ 7, 8, 17, 18, 21). On the other hand, the anthropological *Weltanschauung,* and indeed only the anthropological *Weltanschauung,* succeeds in negating the theological viewpoint completely, that is, in both its meanings.

Section 58 really brings to a conclusion the argument in favor of "the new philosophy" as contrasted with Hegelian speculative philosophy. The work could have ended appropriately at this point; but, interestingly enough, Feuerbach does not end on this note. The last seven sections, which are short epigrams, introduce a new theme: the truth lies, not in the solitary, concrete man, but in the community of concrete men, between man and man.

> The single man for himself possesses the essence of man neither in himself as a moral being nor in himself as a thinking being. The essence of man is contained only in the community and unity of man with man. . . . (§ 59)

Solitude is finiteness and limitation; community is freedom and infinity (§ 60).

> It is the truth that no being—be it man, God, mind, or ego—is for itself alone a true, perfect, and absolute being, that truth and perfection are only the connection and unity of beings equal in their essence. The highest and last principle of philosophy is, therefore, the unity of man with man. (§ 63)

Feuerbach does not develop and elaborate this theme in the *Principles.* He merely enunciates it in a few short sections. The language of these sections is striking and charged with emotion. Thus the closing sections provide a fitting climax to the work. The curious thing is, however, that Feuerbach ends the *Principles* on a note that is sympathetic to religion. This is in marked contrast to Feuerbach's attitude throughout the rest of the work. In all the many instances that God and religion are mentioned in the *Principles* the only two where they are referred to positively occur in the last seven sections. In § 60, Feuerbach says: "man with man–the unity of I and thou–is God." And, in § 64–which is really the last section of the work in which Feuerbach deals with substantive material, § 65 being merely a repetitious summation–Feuerbach ends by equating "the new philosophy" with religion. "It ["the new philosophy"] takes the place of religion and has the essence of religion within itself; in truth, it is itself religion."

The *Principles* seems to have been intended as a work critical of abstract, rational theology. As long as Feuerbach is considering only abstract, rational theology, his position is consistently negative and critical. In the last seven sections, he moves to complete his anthropological viewpoint, and here it is no longer abstract, rational theology that is involved, but the wider aspect of religion. It will not do to equate Feuerbach's position toward religion in general with his position toward abstract, rational theology. His position toward religion is much more involved and, in the last analysis, ambiguous and questionable. Here is not the incisive and clear-cut negation found in him when abstract, rational theology is involved. With respect to abstract, rational theology, "the new philosophy" is its complete dissolution. With respect to religion, it is its essence: "In truth, it is itself religion."

This is, then, the thematic structure of the *Principles*. Although it is complex, it is nevertheless held tightly together as a thematic unit. Everything proceeds toward the basic thesis of the work–the establishing of "the new philosophy." The involution of the structure results from Feuerbach's desire to establish "the new philosophy" on two levels. On the one level, he sees "the new philosophy" as the expression of a *Weltanschauung* that diametrically opposes the *Weltanschauung* of the modern era. The argument must, therefore, proceed to negate the antithetical *Weltanschauung* and affirm the *Weltanschauung* of "the new philosophy." On the second level, Feuerbach wants to establish "the new philosophy" as the continuation and, indeed, the successful culmination of the modern era. "The new philosophy" expresses what the modern era really wanted and attempted to say. The argument here must uncover the seeds of "the new philosophy" in the modern era. Thus, two lines of argumentation run side by side. They meet in "the new philosophy," but in the analysis of the modern era they run counter to each other. The first line of argument is negative and destructive; the second line is positive and constructive. Because both lines continuously crisscross each other throughout the work, the reader may well find the task of following Feuerbach's thought a challenge. It is a challenge, however, that has in store great rewards for those who meet it.

MANFRED H. VOGEL

Selected Bibliography

FEUERBACH EDITIONS

Sämmtliche Werke. 10 vols. Leipzig, 1846–1866.

Sämtliche Werke. Ed. W. BOLIN and F. JODL. 10 vols. Stuttgart: Frommanns Verlag, 1903–1911.

Sämtliche Werke. Ed. W. BOLIN and F. JODL. Stuttgart: Frommanns Verlag. Vols. I–X republished 1960 with introduction by K. LÖWITH. Vols. XI–XIII, ed. H. M. SASS, contain Feuerbach's thesis in original Latin, the facsimile-reprint of 1830 edition of the *Thoughts on Death and Immortality,* and complete German Bibliography (Vol. XI). Vols. XII–XIII are republication of the *Ausgewählte Briefe,* ed. W. BOLIN.

Ausgewählte Briefe. Ed. W. BOLIN. 2 vols. Leipzig, 1904. K. GRÜN. 2 vols. Leipzig, 1874.

Briefwechsel zwischen Feuerbach und C. Kapp. Ed. A. KAPP. Leipzig, 1876.

Ludwig Feuerbachs Philosophie der Zukunft. Ed., with Introduction, by H. EHRENBURG. Stuttgart, 1914.

Das Wesen des Christentums. Ed., with Introduction, by W. SCHUFFENHAUER. Berlin: Academie-Verlag, 1956.

The Essence of Christianity. Trans. M. EVANS, G. ELIOT, and C. BLANCHARD. New York, 1855. Reprinted, New York: Harper Torchbooks, 1957, with introductory essay by K. BARTH, trans. J. L. ADAMS, and Foreword by R. NIEBUHR.

CRITICAL WORKS ON FEUERBACH

ARVON. *Ludwig Feuerbach ou la Transformation du Sacre.* Paris, 1957.

BOCKMÜHL, K. E. *Leiblichkeit und gesellschaft.* Göttingen, 1961.

CHAMBERLAIN, W. B. *Heaven Wasn't His Destination.* London, 1941.

DICKE, G. *Der Identitätsgedanke bei Feuerbach und Marx.* Cologne, 1960.

ENGELS, F. *Ludwig Feuerbach and the Outcome of Classical German Philosophy.* New York: International Publishers, 1934.

NUEDLING, G. *Ludwig Feuerbachs Religionsphilosophie.* Paderborn, 1936.

RAWIDOWICZ, S. *Ludwig Feuerbachs Philosophie.* Berlin, 1931.

SCHILLING, W. *Feuerbach und die Religion.* Munich, 1955.

SCHUFFENHAUER, W. *Ludwig Feuerbach.* Berlin, 1958.

GENERAL

BARTH, K. *Protestant Thought.* Trans. B. COZENS; rev. trans. H. H. HARTWELL. New York: Harper, 1959.

———. *Theology and Church.* Trans. L. P. SMITH. New York: Harper, 1962.

———. *Church Dogmatics.* Vol. IV. Zürich, 1955.

BUBER, M. *Between Man and Man.* Edinburgh, 1947.

HIRSCH, E. *Geschichte der neueren evangelischen Theologie.* Vol. V. Gütersloh, 1954.

HOOK, S. *From Hegel to Marx.* New York: Humanities Press, 1950.

HUCH, R. *Alte und Neue Gotter.* Berlin, 1930.

KOIGEN, D. *Der Moralische Got.* Berlin, 1922.

LÖWITH, K. *Von Hegel zu Nietzsche.* Stuttgart, 1941.

LUBAC, H. DE. *Die Tragödie des Humanismus ohne Gott.* Salzburg, 1950.

MARCUSE, H. *Reason and Revolution.* New York: Humanities Press, 1941, 1955.

MARX, K. and F. ENGELS. *The German Ideology,* Parts I and III. New York: International Publishers, 1939.

MAUTHNER, F. *Der Atheismus und seine Geschichte in Abendlande.* Vol. IV. Stuttgart, 1923.

POPPER-LYNKEUS, J. *Über Religion*. Vienna, 1924.
REDING, M. *Der politische Atheismus*. Graz, 1957.
TUCKER, R. *Philosophy and Myth in Karl Marx*. New York: Cambridge University Press, 1961.

PRINCIPLES OF THE PHILOSOPHY OF THE FUTURE

Preface to the First Edition

These principles contain the continuation and further justification of my *Thesen zur Reform der Philosophie,* which was banned by the most arbitrary decree of the German censors. According to the first manuscript, these principles were intended to lead to a detailed book; but, when I reached the phase of making a fine copy, I was seized—I myself do not know how—by the spirit of the German censors, and I cut it like a barbarian. What remained from this indiscreet censorship was reduced to the following few pages.

I called them *Principles of the Philosophy of the Future* because generally the present era, as an era of refined illusions and priggish prejudices, is incapable of understanding, not to speak of appreciating, the simple truths from which these principles are abstracted—precisely because of their simplicity.

The philosophy of the future has the task of leading philosophy from the realm of "departed souls" back into the realm of embodied and living souls; of pulling philosophy down from the divine, self-sufficient bliss in the realm of ideas into human misery. To this end, it needs nothing more than human understanding and human speech. To think, speak, and act in a pure and true human fashion will, however, be granted only to future generations. At present, the task is not to present man as such, but to pull him out of the mud in which he has been embedded. These principles are the fruit of this unsavory work of cleansing. The task of these principles was to derive the necessity of a philosophy of man, that is, of anthropology, from the philosophy of the absolute, that is, theology, and to establish the critique of human philosophy through the critique of divine philosophy. Thus, these principles presuppose, for their evaluation, a close familiarity with the philosophy of the modern era.

The consequences of these principles will certainly follow.

Bruckberg
July 9, 1843

Principles of the Philosophy of the Future

1

The task of the modern era was the realization and humanization of God—the transformation and dissolution of theology into anthropology.

2

The religious or practical form of this humanization was Protestantism. The God who is man, the human God, namely, Christ—only this is the God of Protestantism. Protestantism is no longer concerned, as Catholicism is, about what God is in himself, but about what he is for man; it has, therefore, no longer a speculative or contemplative tendency, as is the case in Catholicism. It is no longer theology; it is essentially Christology, that is, religious anthropology.

3

God in himself, or God as God—for God in himself is only then essentially God—was, however, negated by Protestantism only in a practical way; theoretically, it left him untouched. He exists, but not for the religious man. He is a transcendent being that will become an object for man only when he is in Heaven. But what lies in the other world for religion lies in this world for philosophy; what is no object for the former is precisely the object for the latter.

4

Speculative philosophy is the rational or theoretical elaboration and dissolution of God, who is, for religion, otherworldly.

5

The essence of speculative philosophy is nothing but the rationalized, realized, presented essence of God. Speculative philosophy is the true, consistent, and rational theology.

6

God as God—as an intellectual or abstracted being, that is, a nonhuman, nonsensuous being that is an object only of reason or intelligence and is accessible only to them—is nothing but the essence of reason itself. He is, however, conceived by ordinary theology or theism by means of the imagination as a being distinct from and independent of reason. It is, therefore, an intrinsic and holy necessity that the essence of reason—which is now separated from it—be finally identified with reason, that the divine being be recognized as the being of reason and be realized and presented as such. On this necessity rests the paramount historical significance of speculative philosophy.

The proof that the divine being is the being of reason or of intellect lies in the fact that the determinations or attributes of God—insofar, of course, as they are rational or intellectual—are not determinations of sensation or of the imagination, but attributes of reason.

"God is the infinite being, the being without any limitation." But that which is not a boundary or a limit for God is also not a limit for reason. Where, for instance, God is a being elevated above the limits of sensation, there also, surpassing those limits, is reason. Whoever can think of no other being but a sensuous being, whoever therefore possesses a reason limited by sensation, will, precisely as a result, also have a God limited by sensation. That reason that conceives of God as an unlimited being conceives of God only its own limitlessness. That which is a divine being for reason is also the truly reasonable being for it—that is, the being that is completely congruent with reason and, therefore, precisely satisfies it. However, that in which a being finds its satisfaction is nothing other than its objectified being. He who satisfies himself through a poet is himself of a poetic nature; he who satisfies himself through a philosopher is himself of a philosophical nature; and the fact that he is this becomes only in the moment of satisfaction an object for him and others. Reason, "however, does not stop at sensuous and finite objects; it satisfies itself only in the infinite being." Thus, the essence of reason is disclosed to us only in this being.

"God is necessary being." But his necessity rests on the fact that he is a rational, intelligent being. The world, that is, matter, does not contain the cause of its being nor of the way it exists in itself; the world is completely indifferent to whether it exists, to whether it exists thus or otherwise.[1] Thus, the world necessarily presupposes another being as cause and, indeed, an understanding, a self-conscious being that acts according to reasons and purposes. For, if intelligence is taken away from this other being, the question is raised anew as to its cause. The necessity of the primary, highest being rests, therefore, on the presupposition that the understanding alone is the primary, highest, necessary, and true being. Just as, in general, the metaphysical or ontotheological determinations first assume truth and reality when they are traced back to psychological or, rather, anthropological determinations, so also the necessity of the divine being in the old metaphysics or ontotheology first assumes meaning and understanding, truth and reality, in the psychological or anthropological determination of God as an intelligent being. The necessary being is the being that necessitates its being thought, that is

[1] It is self-understood that here, as in all other sections where historical material is involved and developed, I do not speak and argue from my point of view, but rather in the name of the historical point of view represented. Thus, here I speak for theism.

simply affirmed, simply undeniable or indestructible—but only as a self-thinking being. In this necessary being, therefore, reason proves and demonstrates only its own necessity and reality.

"God is unconditional, general—'God is not this or that' —immutable, eternal, or timeless being." But absoluteness, immutability, eternity, and generality are themselves, according to the judgment of metaphysical theology, also attributes of the truths or laws of reason, consequently attributes of reason itself; for what are these unalterable, general, unconditioned truths of reason that are valid always and everywhere if not expressions of the essence of reason?

"God is independent, self-sufficient being who needs no other being for his own being, consequently existing by and through himself." But here, too, this abstract, metaphysical determination has meaning and reality only as a definition of the essence of reason and states, therefore, nothing but that God is a thinking, intelligent being or conversely that only a thinking being is divine; for only a sensuous being needs other, external objects for its being. I do need air in order to breathe, water to drink, light to see, vegetable and animal materials to eat; but nothing, at least directly, in order to think. I cannot conceive of a breathing being without air, a seeing being without light, but I can conceive of a thinking being isolated in itself. That being that breathes necessarily relates itself to a being external to itself and has its essential object through which it is what it is outside itself; but a thinking being relates to itself, being its own object, having its essence in itself, and being what it is through itself.

7

That which is object in theism is subject in speculative philosophy; what in the former is only the conceived and imagined being of reason is in the latter the thinking being of reason itself.

The theist conceives God as an existing and personal being

external to reason and in general apart from man; he, as subject, thinks about God as an object. He conceives God as a being; namely, according to his imagination, God is a spiritual and unsensuous being, but, in accordance with actuality, that is, with the truth, he is a sensuous being; for the essential characteristic of an objective being, of a being outside thoughts or the imagination, is sensation. He distinguishes God from himself in the same way in which he distinguishes sensuous objects and beings as existing apart from him; in short, he conceives God from the point of view of sensation. The speculative theologian or philosopher, on the other hand, conceives God from the point of view of thought. He therefore does not have the disturbing appearance of a sensuous being midway between him and God. He thus identifies, without any hindrance, the objective, conceived being with the subjective, thinking being.

The intrinsic necessity by which God changes from an object of man to his subject, to his thinking ego, can be derived more precisely from that which was already expounded in the following way. God is an object of man, and only of man; he is not an object of animals. The essence of a being is recognized, however, only through its object; the object to which a being is necessarily related is nothing but its own revealed being. Thus, the object of herbivorous animals is the plant; however, by means of this object they essentially differentiate themselves from the other animals, the carnivorous ones. Thus, the object of the eye is neither tone nor smell, but light. In the object of the eye, however, its essence is revealed to us. It is, therefore, irrelevant whether one cannot see or does not possess an eye. We therefore also name in life things and beings only according to their objects. The eye is "the light organ." He who cultivates the soil is a farmer; he who makes hunting the object of his activity is a hunter; he who catches fish is a fisherman; and so on. If, now, God is an object of man—and, indeed, inasmuch as he really is a necessary and essential object—what is expressed in the being of this object is merely the peculiar essence of man. Imagine to yourself a thinking being on a planet or even a comet seeing a few paragraphs of Christian dogmatics dealing with the being of God. What would this being conclude from these paragraphs? Perhaps the existence of a god in the sense of Christian dogmatics? No! it would infer only that there are thinking beings also on earth; it would find in the definitions of the earth inhabitants regarding their god only definitions of their own being. For example, in the definition 'God is a spirit' it would find only the proof and expression of their own spirit; in short, the essence and attributes of the subject would be derived from the essence and attributes of the object. And rightly so, for the distinction between what the object is in itself and what it is for man is removed in the case of this object. This distinction is only justifiable in the case of a directly sensed object, which is precisely, therefore, an object also of beings apart from man. Light exists not only for man, but it affects also animals, plants, and inorganic substances: it is a general entity. In order to find what light is, we consider, therefore, not only its impact and effects on us, but also on other beings distinct from us. The distinction between the object in itself and the object for us—namely, between the object in reality and the object in our thought and imagination—is therefore necessarily and objectively grounded here. God is, however, only an object of man. Animals and stars praise God only in the mind of man. It is, thus, an innate characteristic of God's own essence that he is an object of no being other than man, that he is a specifically human object, a secret of man. But, if God is only an object of man, what is revealed to us in his essence? Nothing but the essence of man. That whose object is the highest being is itself the highest being. The more of man animals assume as an object, the higher they rank and the closer they approach man. An animal whose object were man as man, the essential human being, would no longer be an animal but itself man. Only equal beings—and, indeed, as they are in themselves—are objects for one another. The identity of the divine and human being is, to be sure, known also to theism. But, because the theist conceives God as a sensuous being existing apart from man—disregarding the fact that at the same time he places the essence of God in the spirit—this identity is for him also an object, but only as a sensuous identity, as similarity or kinship. Kinship expresses the same relationship as identity; but at the same time kinship is bound to the sensuous imagination by which the related beings are made into two independent, that is, sensuous, beings existing apart from each other.

8

Ordinary theology transforms the point of view of man into the point of view of God; speculative theology, on the other hand, transforms the point of view of God into the point of view of man or, rather, of the thinker.

For ordinary theology, God is an object and, indeed, an object just like any other sensuous object; but, at the same time, he is also for ordinary theology a subject, just like the human subject. God creates things that are apart from him, relates himself to himself and to other beings that exist apart from him, loves and thinks himself and other beings at the same time. In short, man transforms his thoughts and even his emotions into thoughts and emotions of God, his essence and his viewpoint into the essence and viewpoint of God. Speculative theology, however, reverses this. Hence, in ordinary theology, God is self-contradictory, for he is supposed to be a nonhuman and superhuman being; yet in truth he is—according to all his determinations—a human being. In speculative theology or philosophy, on the other hand, God is in contradiction to man; he is supposed to be the essence of man, at least of reason, and yet in truth he is a nonhuman and superhuman, that is, abstracted being. In ordinary theology, the superhuman God is only imaginary, an edifying cliché and a toy of fantasy; in speculative philosophy, on the other hand, he is truth and bitter seriousness. The severe contradiction in which speculative philosophy became involved was caused only by the fact that it made God—who in theism is only a being of fantasy, a far-removed, indefinite, and cloudy being—into a present and definite being, thus destroying the illusive charm that a being far removed has in the blue haze of the imagination. Thus, the theists were much upset over the fact that, according to Hegel, logic is supposed to be the presentation of God in his eternal, preworldly essence, and yet, for example, in the section on quantity, it deals with extensive and intensive quantity, fractions, powers, and proportions. What, they cried out, should this God be our God? And yet this God is nothing but the God of theism who is drawn out of the fog of the indefinite imagination into the light of definite thought, the God of theism, so to speak, taken at his word of having created and ordered everything according to measure, number, and weight. If God has ordered and created all according to quantity and measure, then measure and quantity before they were realized in things existing apart from God were—and still are—in the mind and consequently in the essence of God, for there is no difference between the mind of God and his essence. Does, then, mathematics not also belong to the mysteries of theology? But, of course, a being appears quite different in fancy and imagination than in truth and reality; no wonder that one and the same being appears to those who only follow mere appearance and semblance as two completely distinct beings.

9

The essential attributes or predicates of the divine being are the essential attributes or predicates of speculative philosophy.

10

God is pure spirit, pure essence, and pure action (*actus purus*), without passion, external determination, sensation, or matter. Speculative philosophy is this pure spirit and pure activity realized as an act of thought—the absolute being as absolute thought.

By the same token that abstraction from all that is sensuous and material was once the necessary condition of theology, so was it also the necessary condition of speculative philosophy, except for the difference that the theological abstraction was, as it were, a sensuous abstraction, because its object, although reached by abstraction, was at the same time imagined as a sensuous being, whereas the abstraction of speculative philosophy is an intellectual and ideated abstraction that has only scientific or theoretical, but not practical, meaning. The beginning of Descartes' philosophy, namely, the abstraction from sensation and matter, is the beginning of modern speculative philosophy. However, Descartes and Leibniz considered this abstraction merely as a subjective condition in order to know the immaterial, divine being; they conceived the immateriality of God as an objective attribute independent of abstraction and thought; they still shared the viewpoint of theism in conceiving the immaterial being only as an object, but not as a subject, as the active principle and real essence of philosophy. To be sure, God is also in Descartes and Leibniz the principle of philosophy, but only as an object distinct from thought and therefore a principle only in general and in the imagination, but not in actuality and truth. God is only the prime and general cause of matter, motion, and activity; but particular motions and activities and specific, real, and material objects are considered and known as independent of God. Leibniz and Descartes are idealists only in general, but specifically they are materialists. Only God is the consistent, complete, and true idealist, for only he conceives all things without obscurity, that is, without the senses and the imagination (according to the meaning of Leibniz' philosophy). He is pure mind, that is, mind that is separated from all that is sensuous and material; material things are for him, therefore, pure entities of the mind and pure thought-objects; for him, matter does not exist at all, because it rests on obscure, that is, sensuous conceptions. But, at the same time, man, too, in Leibniz' philosophy, has already in himself a good portion of idealism, for in addition to his senses and imagination he has mind; and mind, precisely because it is a thinking being, is an immaterial, pure being. How would it have been possible for one to conceive an immaterial being without an immaterial faculty and consequently without having immaterial conceptions? But man's mind is not so completely pure, in its absoluteness or in its range, as the mind or being of God. Man, or, rather, this man Leibniz, is thus a partial or semi-idealist, and only God is a complete idealist, "the perfect sage" (*der volkommene Weltweise*), as he is expressly called by Wolf. That means that God is the idea of the perfect, elaborate, absolute idealism of later speculative philosophy. For what is the mind or, generally, the being of God? It is nothing other than the mind and being of man separated from the determinations—be they real or assumed—that at certain times are bounds on man. He who does not have a mind that is torn asunder from the senses and who does not view the senses as bounds also does not view a mind without the senses as the highest and true intellect. What is, however, the idea of a thing if not its essence purified of the limitation and obscurity that it suffers in reality where it is related to other things? Thus, according to Leibniz, the limitation of the human mind lies in the fact that it is fixed to materialism, that is, obscure conceptions; these obscure conceptions arise only because the human being is related to other beings and to the world in general. But this relationship does not belong to the essence of the mind; rather, it contradicts the mind, for the mind in itself, that is, in the idea, is an immaterial being, that is, a being existing for itself and isolated. And this idea, or this mind, that is purified of all materialistic conceptions is precisely the divine mind. What was, however, merely an idea with Leibniz became truth and reality in later philosophy. Absolute idealism is nothing but the realized divine mind of Leibnizian theism; it is the pure mind systematically elaborated, which divests all things of their sensuousness, transforming them into pure entities of the mind, into thought-objects; it is the pure mind unattached to any foreign features, concerned only with itself as the essence of essences.

11

God is a thinking being; but the objects that he thinks and comprehends are, like his mind, not distinguished from his being. Thus, in thinking the objects, he thinks only himself, namely, he remains in an unbroken unity with himself. This unity of thought and the objects of thought is, however, the secret of speculative thought.

So, for example, in Hegel's *Logic* the objects of thought are not distinguished from the essence of thought. Thought stays here in an unbroken unity with itself! Its objects are only determinations of thought. They dissolve completely into it and keep for themselves nothing that would have remained outside the thought process. But that which is the essence of logic is also the essence of God. God is a spiritual, abstracted being; at the same time, however, he is the essence of being that embraces all beings in itself in unity with his abstracted being. But what are these beings that are identical to an abstracted, spiritual being? They themselves are abstracted beings–ideas. Things when existing in God are not the same as when they exist apart from him; they differ from real things to the same extent that things that are objects of logic differ from things that are the objects of real perception. To what, then, is the difference between divine and metaphysical thought reduced? Just to a difference of imagination, to a difference between thought that is merely imagined and real thought.

12

The difference between God's knowledge or thought, which as an archetype precedes the objects and creates them, and man's knowledge, which follows the objects as their copy, is nothing but the difference between a priori, or speculative, knowledge and a posteriori, or empirical, knowledge. Although theism conceives God as a thinking or a spiritual being, at the same time it conceives him as a sensuous being. It directly links, therefore, sensuous and material effects with the thinking and willing of God. These effects contradict the essence of thought and will and express nothing more than the power of nature. Such a material effect—consequently, a mere expression of sensuous power—is above all the creation or the bringing forth of the real and material world. Speculative theology, on the other hand, transforms this sensuous act, which contradicts the essence of thought, into a logical or theoretical act, thus transforming the material creation of the object into the speculative generation of the idea. In theism, the world is a temporal product of God; the world has existed for a few thousand years, and before it came into being there was God. In speculative theology, on the other hand, the world or nature is subsequent to God only according to rank and significance; accident presupposes substance and nature presupposes logic. This is according to the idea, but not according to sensuous existence and consequently not according to time.

Theism, however, attributes to God not only speculative but also—and indeed in its highest perfection—sensuous and empirical knowledge. By the same token that the preworldly and preobjective knowledge of God found its realization, truth, and reality in the a priori knowledge of speculative philosophy, so did the sensuous knowledge of God find its realization, truth, and reality in the empirical sciences of the modern era. The most perfect, and hence divine, sensuous knowledge is indeed nothing other than the most sensuous knowledge that knows the most minute objects and the least noticeable details, that knows the hair on man's head not by grasping it indiscriminately in one lock but by counting them, thus knowing them all, hair by hair. "God is therefore the all-knowing," says St. Thomas Aquinas, "because he knows the most particular things." But this divine knowledge, which is only an imaginary conception and a fantasy in theology, became rational and real knowledge in the knowledge of the natural sciences gained through the telescope and microscope.

It counted the stars in the sky, the ova in the spawn of fish and butterflies, and the color spots on the wings of insects in order to distinguish them from one another; it alone demonstrated anatomically in the grub of the butterfly 288 muscles in the head, 1,647 in the body, and 2,186 in the stomach and intestines. What more can one ask? We have here an apparent example of the truth that man's conception of God is the human individual's conception of his own species, that God as the total of all realities or perfections is nothing other than the total of the attributes of the species—dispersed among men and realizing themselves in the course of world history—compendiously combined for the benefit of the limited individual. The domain of the natural sciences is, because of its quantitative size, completely beyond the capacity of the individual man to view and measure. Who is able to count the stars in the sky and at the same time the muscles and nerves in the body of the caterpillar? Lyonnet lost his sight over the anatomy of the caterpillar. Who is able to observe simultaneously the differences of height and depth on the moon and at the same time observe the differences of the innumerable ammonites and terebrates? But what the individual man does not know and cannot do all of mankind together knows and can do. Thus, the divine knowledge that knows simultaneously every particular has its reality in the knowledge of the species.

Not only divine omniscience but also divine omnipresence has realized itself in man. While one man notices what is happening on the moon or Uranus, another observes Venus or the intestines of the caterpillar or some other place that no human eye—while it was under the lordship of an omniscient and omnipresent God—has ever seen before. Indeed, while one man observes this star from the position of Europe, another observes the same star from the position of America. What is absolutely impossible for one man alone to accomplish is possible for two men to achieve. But God is in all places and knows all at the same time without distinction. Granted; but one should note that this omniscience and omnipresence exist only in the imagination and in fancy, and one should not overlook the important difference, which has already been mentioned several times, between that which is only imagined and the real object. In the imagination, to be sure, one can view the 4,059 muscles of a caterpillar with one look; in reality, however, where they exist apart from one another they can be viewed only one after the other. Thus, the limited individual can also in his imagination conceive of the range of human knowledge as finite, although, if he really wanted to appropriate this knowledge, he would never reach its end. Let one take as an example just one science, history, for instance, and dissolve in thought world history into the histories of single countries, these into the histories of single provinces, these again into chronicles of cities, and the chronicles into histories of families and biographies. When would a single man ever reach the point where he could exclaim: "Here I am at the end of the historical knowledge of mankind!"? Thus also, our life span, both the past as well as the possible future, even when greatly extended, appears to us in the imagination extraordinarily short. In moments when we thus imagine our life, we feel compelled to extend and complete by an immeasurable and endless life after death that which in our imagination is but the disappearing brevity of our life. But how long in reality does a day last, or just one hour! Whence this difference? The answer emerges from the following: time in the imagination is empty time, namely, a nothing between the beginning and the end of our calculation; the real life span, however, is fulfilled time, where mountains of all kinds of difficulties lie midway between the now and the then.

13

The absolute absence of all premises—namely, the beginning of speculative philosophy—is nothing other than the lack of premise and beginning, the aseity of the divine being. Theology distinguishes between active and passive attributes of God. Philosophy, however, also transforms the passive attributes into active ones—the entire being of God into action, which, however, is human action. This is also valid regarding the predicate of this paragraph. Philosophy presupposes nothing; this is nothing more than to say that it abstracts from all objects given immediately, that is, objects given in sensation and thus distinguished from objects given in thought. In short, it abstracts from everything from which it is possible to abstract without stopping to think, and makes this act of abstracting from all objectivity the beginning of itself. What is, however, the absolute being if not the being for which nothing is to be presupposed and to which no object apart from itself is given and is necessary? What is it if not the being removed from all objects, from all sensuous things distinct and distinguishable from itself? What is it if not the being that, therefore, also becomes an object for man only through an abstraction from all these things? That from which God is free, from that you must liberate yourself if you want to reach God; and you make yourself really free when you conceive him. Consequently, if you think of God as a being that does not presuppose any other beings or objects, then you yourself will also think without presupposing an external object; the attribute that you affix to God is an attribute of your thought. Only what is activity in man is being in God or imagined as such. What, then, is the ego of Fichte that says, "I simply am because I am," or the pure, presuppositionless thought of Hegel if not the divine being of the old theology and metaphysics transformed into the present, active, and thinking being of man?

14

Speculative philosophy as the realization of God is at the same time the positing and the cancellation or negation of God, at the same time theism and atheism; for God, in the theological sense, is God only as long as he is conceived as a being distinguished from and independent of the being of man and nature. Theism that as the positing of God is at the same time the negation of God—or conversely as the negation of God is at the same time still the affirmation of God—is pantheism. Actual or theological theism is, however, nothing other than imaginary pantheism; imaginary pantheism is nothing other than real, true theism.

That which separates theism from pantheism is only the conception or the imagining of God as a personal being. All the determinations of God—and God is necessarily determined, otherwise he is nothing, not even an object of the imagination—are determinations of reality—of nature, of man, or of both. Hence, they are pantheistic determinations, for that which does not distinguish God from the being of nature or of man is pantheism. God is thus distinguished from the world, from the totality of nature and mankind, only by his personality or existence, but not by his determinations or his essence; that is, he is only imagined as a different being, but in truth he is not a different being. Theism is the contradiction of appearance and essence, imagination and truth, whereas pantheism is the unity of both; pantheism is the naked truth of theism. All the conceptions of theism, when grasped, seriously considered, carried out, and realized, lead necessarily to pantheism. Pantheism is consistent theism. Theism thinks of God as the cause—and indeed as a living and personal cause—and the creator of the world; God has brought forth the world by his will. But the will does not suffice. Where there is once will, there must also be mind; that which one wills is a matter of the mind. Without mind, there is no object. The things that God created existed, therefore, before their creation in God as objects of his mind, as entities of the mind. The mind of God is, it is said in theology, the total of all things and essences. Where else would they have sprung from, if not from nothingness? And it is irrelevant whether you conceive this nothingness in your imagination as independent or place it in God. But God contains, or is, everything only in an ideal manner, in the manner of the imagination. This ideal pantheism, however, leads necessarily to the real or the actual; for it is not far from God's mind to his being nor from his being to his reality. How could the mind allow itself to be separated from the being, and how could the being allow itself to be separated from the reality or existence of God? If the objects are in God's mind, how could they be apart from his being? If they are the outcome of his mind, why not the outcome of his being? If in God his being is directly identical with his reality and if God's existence is inseparable from the concept of God, how could the conception of the object and the real object be separated in God's conception of things? How, then, could the difference between the object in the conception and the object apart from the conception, which constitutes only the nature of the finite and nondivine mind, take place in God? But, once we have no more objects apart from God's mind, so we soon will also have no more objects apart from his being and finally apart from his existence. All objects are in God, and indeed in truth and actuality, not only in the imagination; for, when the objects are only in the imagination—of God as well as of man—namely, when they are merely ideal or rather imaginary in God, then they exist at the same time outside the imagination, outside God. But, if we were once to have no more objects and no world apart from God, so would we also have no more God—not only an ideal and imagined, but a real, being—apart from the world. In a word, we have Spinozism or pantheism.

Theism conceives God as a purely immaterial being. To determine God as immaterial, however, means nothing else than to determine matter as a thing of nothingness, as a nonbeing, for only God is the measure of reality. Only God is being, truth, and essence; only what is valid in and through God has being; what is denied of God has no being. To derive matter from God means, therefore, nothing other than the wish to prove the being of matter by its nonbeing, for derivation is the indication of a ground and a justification. God made matter. But how, why, and from what? To this, theism gives no answer. Matter for theism is a purely inexplicable existence; that is, it is the limit, the end of theology on which it is wrecked in life as well as in thought. How can I, then, derive the end and negation of theology from theology without negating it? How can I look for explanation and information when theology's intelligence fails? How can I, from the negation of matter or the world, which is the essence of theology, from the proposition "matter does not exist," deduce—and, indeed, despite the God of theology—the affirmation of matter, the proposition "matter exists"? How else, but with mere fictions. Material things can only be derived from God, if God himself is determined as a material being. Only so will God change from an imagined and fancied cause into the real cause of the world. He who is not ashamed to make shoes should also not be ashamed to be and be called a shoemaker. Hans Sachs was, indeed, a shoemaker as well as a poet. But the shoes were the work of his hands, whereas his poems were the work of his mind. As the effect is, so is the cause. But matter is not God; it is, rather, the finite, the nondivine, the negation of God. The absolute admirers and followers of matter are atheists. Pantheism connects, therefore, atheism with theism, the negation of God with God; God is a material or, in the language of Spinoza, an extended being.

15

Pantheism is theological atheism or theological materialism. It is but the negation of theology on the grounds of theology, for it makes matter, which is the negation of God, into a predicate or attribute of the divine being. However, he who makes matter into an attribute of God declares matter to be a divine being. The realization of God presupposes in general the divinity, that is, the truth and essentiality, of the real. The divinization of the real, of that which exists materially—materialism, empiricism, realism, humanism—and the negation of theology are, however, the essence of the modern era. Pantheism is, therefore, nothing other than the essence of the modern era elevated to a divine being and to a religiophilosophical principle.

Empiricism or realism—by which is here understood generally the so-called real sciences, especially the natural sciences—

negates theology. It is, however, not a theoretical but a practical negation; it is a negation by means of the act through which the realist makes that which is the negation of God, or at least is not God, into the essential business of his life and the essential object of his activity. He, however, who concentrates with heart and mind on the material and sensuous only, actually denies the supernatural its reality; for only that is real, at least for man, that is an object of true and real activity. "What I don't know doesn't hurt me." The statement that one cannot know anything of the supernatural is only an excuse. God and divine things are no longer known only when one does not want to know them. How much was known of God, of the devils, or of the angels as long as these supernatural beings were still objects of a real faith! That in which one is interested is also the thing in which one is proficient. The mystics and scholastics of the Middle Ages had no ability and aptitude for natural science only because they had no interest in nature. Wherever the disposition is not lacking, there also the senses and organs are not lacking. That to which the heart is open is also accessible to the mind. Thus, mankind in the modern era lost the organs for the supernatural world and its secrets only because it lost together with the faith also the disposition toward the supernatural world, because its essential tendency was anti-Christian and antitheological; that is, it was an anthropological, cosmic, realistic, and materialistic tendency.[1] Spinoza hit the nail on the head, therefore, with his paradoxical proposition: God is an extended, that is, material being. He found, at least for his time, the true philosophic expression for the materialistic tendency of the modern era; he legitimized and sanctioned it: God himself is a materialist. Spinoza's philosophy was religion; he himself was a remarkable person. With him, materialism was not, as it was with so many others, in contradiction to the conception of an immaterial and antimaterialistic God who consequently also orders only antimaterialistic, heavenly tendencies and activities as

1 The differences between materialism, empiricism, realism, and humanism are in this work irrelevant.

duties for man. For God is nothing other than the original and the model of man; corresponding to how God is and what he is man must be and wants to be or at least hopes to be in the future. But only where theory does not deny practice and practice does not deny theory is there character, truth, and religion. Spinoza is the Moses of modern freethinkers and materialists.

16

Pantheism is the negation of theoretical theology; empiricism is the negation of practical theology. Pantheism negates the principle, whereas empiricism negates the consequences of theology.

Pantheism makes God into a present, real, and material being; empiricism, to which rationalism also belongs, makes God into an absent, far-removed, unreal, and negative being. Empiricism does not deny God existence. But it denies him all positive determinations because their content is only finite and empirical; the infinite cannot, therefore, be an object for man. The more attributes, however, I deny to a being, the more I set it apart from myself, the less power and influence I let it exercise on me, the freer I become of it. The more qualities I have, the more I am also for others, the greater is the circumference of my effects and influence. And, the more one is, the more one is known. Each negation of an attribute of God is, therefore, a partial atheism, a sphere of godlessness. To the extent that I remove an attribute, I also remove from God his being. If, for example, sympathy and mercy are not attributes of God, then I am alone in my suffering; God is not here as my comforter. If God is the negation of all finiteness, so consequently the finite is also the negation of God. Only if God thinks of me—so concludes the religious man—do I also have reason and cause to think of him; only in his "being for me" lies the cause of my "being for him." For empiricism, therefore, the theological being is in truth nothing any more, that is, nothing real; but it attributes this nonbeing not to the object, but only to itself, to its knowledge. The empiricist does not deny God's being, that is, maintaining God as a dead and indifferent being; but he denies God the being that proves itself as being, that is effective, palpable, and active in life. He affirms God, but negates all the consequences necessarily connected with this affirmation. He repudiates theology and gives it up; yet not for theoretical reasons, but rather because of aversion to, and dislike of the objects of theology, that is, because of an obscure feeling of their unreality. The empiricist thinks to himself that theology is nothing, but he also adds "for me"; that means that his judgment is subjective and pathological. For he does not have the freedom, but also not the desire and the vocation, to bring the objects of theology before the forum of reason. This is the vocation of philosophy. The task of modern philosophy was therefore nothing other than to elevate the pathological judgment of empiricism that there is nothing in theology to a theoretical and objective judgment, to transform the indirect, unconscious, and negative negation of theology into a direct, positive, and conscious negation. How ridiculous it is, therefore, to wish to suppress the "atheism" of philosophy without suppressing at the same time the atheism of experience! How ridiculous it is to persecute the theoretical negation of Christianity and at the same time to let the actual negations of Christianity, in which the modern era abounds, stand as they are! How ridiculous it is to believe that with the consciousness, that is, the symptom, of evil the cause of evil is simultaneously abolished! Indeed, how ridiculous! And yet how rich with such ridiculous things is history! They repeat themselves in all critical periods. No wonder! For, with regard to the past, all is looked on favorably, and the necessity of the changes and revolutions that occurred is acknowledged; its application, however, to the present situation is opposed with every means available. The present is made the exception to the rule because of shortsightedness and complacency.

17

The elevation of matter to a divine being is directly and simultaneously the elevation of reason to a divine being. That which the theist—because of emotional needs and the demand for unlimited bliss—denies God by means of the imagination is affirmed of God by the pantheist because of rational needs. Matter is an essential object of reason. If there were no matter, reason would have no stimulus and substance for thinking and thus no content. Matter cannot be given up without giving up reason; nor can it be acknowledged without acknowledging reason. Materialists are rationalists. Pantheism, however, affirms reason only indirectly as a divine being, namely, by transforming God from a being of imagination, which he is as a personal being in theism, into an object of reason and a being thereof. The direct apotheosis of reason is idealism. Pantheism leads necessarily to idealism. Idealism is related to pantheism in the same way as pantheism is related to theism.

As the object is, so is the subject. According to Descartes, the essence of corporeal things, the body as substance, is not an object of the senses, but only of the mind. But precisely therefore it is also, according to Descartes, not the senses but the mind that is the essence of the perceiving subject, that is, of man. Essence is given as an object only to essence. According to Plato, opinion has as object only impermanent things; therefore, however, it is itself impermanent and changing knowledge—indeed, only opinion. The essence of music is the highest essence to the musician, and, therefore, the ear is to him the highest organ; he would sooner lose his eyes than his ears. The natural scientist, on the other hand, would rather lose his ears than his eyes, because his objective being is light. If I make the tone divine, I also make the ear divine. If I speak like a pantheist, saying that God or, what amounts to the same, absolute being or absolute truth and reality is an object only for and of reason, then I explain God as a rational being or a being of reason and express thereby indirectly only the absolute truth and reality of reason. It is therefore necessary that reason return to itself, reverse this inverted self-recognition, and declare itself directly as the absolute truth, thus becoming directly, without the mediation of another object, its own object as absolute truth. The pantheist says the same thing as the idealist, except that he expresses himself objectively or realistically, whereas the idealist expresses himself subjectively or idealistically. The former has his idealism in the object: apart from substance, apart from God, there is nothing, and all things are only determinations of God. The latter has his pantheism in the ego: apart from the ego, there is nothing, and all things exist only as objects of the ego. But, nevertheless, idealism is the truth of pantheism; this is so because God or substance is only the object of reason, of the ego, and of the thinking being. If I believe or think generally of no God, then by the same token I have no God. He exists for me only through me, and he exists for reason only through reason. The a priori, or first, being is, thus, not the being that is thought, but the thinking being; not the object, but the subject. By the same token that natural science turned necessarily from the light back to the eye, so philosophy necessarily turned from the objects of thinking back to the subject of thinking, that is, the ego. What is light—as the being that brightens and illumines, as the object of optics—without the eye? It is nothing. And thus far goes natural science. But what, philosophy now further asks, is the eye without consciousness? It is also nothing. It is identical whether I see without consciousness or whether I do not see. Only the consciousness of seeing is the reality of seeing or real seeing. But why do you believe that something exists apart from you? Because you see, hear, and feel something. Thus, this something is a real something, a real object only as an object of consciousness; and consciousness is the absolute reality, the measure of all existence. All that exists, exists only as being for consciousness, as comprehended in consciousness; for consciousness is first and foremost being. Thus, the essence of theology realizes itself in idealism, and the essence of God, in the ego and in consciousness. Without God, nothing can exist and nothing can be thought. In terms of idealism, this means that everything exists only as an object, be it a real or a possible object, of consciousness. To exist means to be an object, thus presupposing consciousness. Things, the world in general, are the work and product of an absolute being, of God; but this absolute being is an ego, a conscious and thinking being. Thus, as Descartes, from the viewpoint of theism, so well says, the world is an *Ens rationis divinae,* an idea, a chimera of God. But this idea itself is again only a vague conception in theism and theology. If we, therefore, realize this conception, if we, so to speak, carry out practically what in theism is only theory, then we have the world as a product of the ego (Fichte) or—at least in its appearance and in our intuition of it—as a work or product of our intuition and understanding (Kant). "Nature is derived from the laws of the possibility of experience in general." "The understanding does not derive its laws (a priori) from nature, but rather it prescribes them to it." Kantian idealism, in which the objects conform to the understanding and not the understanding to the objects, is therefore nothing other than the realization of the theological conception of the divine mind, which is not determined by the objects but rather determines them. How silly it is, therefore, to acknowledge idealism in heaven, that is, the idealism of the imagination, as a divine truth, but reject idealism on earth, that is, the idealism of reason, as a human error. Deny idealism and you also deny God! God only is the creator of idealism. If you do not want the consequences, then you also should not want the principle! Idealism is nothing but rational or rationalized theism. But Kant's idealism is still a limited idealism—idealism based on the viewpoint of empiricism. According to what has been said above, God is for empiricism still only a being in conception and in theory—in the ordinary, bad sense—but not in actuality and truth, a thing in itself, but no longer a thing for empiricism, because only empirical and real objects are objects for empiricism. Matter is the only material for its thinking; it has therefore no more matter for God. God exists, but he is for us a *tabula rasa,* an empty being, a mere idea. God, as we conceive and think of him, is our ego, our mind, and our essence; but this God is only an appearance of us and for us, not God in himself. Kant's idealism is the idealism still bound by theism. We often find that, having been freed long ago in actuality from a matter, a doctrine, or an idea, we are at the same time not freed from it in the mind. It is no longer a truth in our existence—perhaps it was never that—but it is still a theoretical truth, a limit on our mind. Mind, because it takes things most thoroughly, is also the last to be free. Theoretical freedom is, at least in many things, the last freedom. How many are republicans in their heart and by their disposition, but in their minds, cannot detach themselves from the monarchy? Their republican hearts are wrecked by the objections and difficulties that the mind presents. So is it also with the theism of Kant. Kant has realized and negated theology in morality and the divine essence in the will. For Kant, the will is the true, original, and unconditional being originating in itself. In actuality, the predicates of the Godhead are claimed by Kant for the will; his theism still has, therefore, only the significance of a theoretical limit. Fichte is a Kant liberated from the limits of theism; he is "the messiah of speculative reason." Fichte's is Kantian idealism, but from the viewpoint of idealism. According to Fichte, the conception of a God who is distinct from us and exists apart from us is given only in the empirical viewpoint. But in truth, from the viewpoint of idealism, the thing in itself, God (since God is the real thing in itself), is only the ego in itself, that is, the ego that is distinct from the individual and empirical ego. Outside the ego, there is no God: "Our religion is reason." But Fichte's idealism is only the negation and realization of abstract and formal theism, of monotheism; it is not the negation and realization of religious and material theism, which is full of content, of trinitarianism, whose realization is "absolute," or Hegelian, idealism. One can put it this way: Fichte has realized the God of pantheism only insofar as he is a thinking being, but not insofar as he is an extended and material being. Fichte's is theistic idealism; Hegel's is pantheistic idealism.

18

Modern philosophy has realized and negated the divine being who is separated and distinguished from sensation, the world, and man. But it realized and negated this divine being only in thought, in reason, and indeed in that reason that is also separated and distinguished from sensation, the world, and man. Namely, modern philosophy has proved only the divinity of mind; it recognized only mind, and indeed the abstract mind, as the divine and absolute being. Descartes' definition of himself as mind, namely, "My essence consists only of the fact that I think," is modern philosophy's definition of itself. The will of Kantian and Fichtean idealism is itself a pure being of the mind; and perception—which Schelling, unlike Fichte, connected with the mind—is only fantasy, untruth, and does not come into consideration.

Modern philosophy proceeded from theology; it is indeed nothing other than theology dissolved and transformed into philosophy. The abstract and transcendental being of God could, therefore, be realized and negated only in an abstract and transcendent way. In order to transform God into reason, reason itself had to assume the quality of an abstract, divine being. The senses, says Descartes, give neither true reality, being, nor certainty; only mind separated from the senses gives truth. Whence this cleavage between the mind and the senses? It is derived only from theology. God is not a sensuous being; he is, rather, the negation of all sensuous determinations and is only known through the abstraction from sensation. But he is God, that is, the truest, the most real, and the most certain being. Whence should truth come to the senses, which are born atheists? God is the being in which existence cannot be separated from essence and concept and which cannot be thought except as existing. Descartes transforms this objective being into a subjective one and the ontological proof into a psychological one; he transforms the proposition, "because God is thinkable, therefore he exists," into the proposition, "I think, therefore I am." As in God there is no separation of being from being thought, so in me—as mind, which is however my essence—being cannot be separated from thought; and, as in the former, so also here this inseparableness constitutes the essence. A being that exists—regardless whether in itself or for me—only as a being of thought, as an object of abstraction from all sensation, necessarily also realizes and subjectifies itself only in a being that exists solely as thought and whose essence is solely abstract thought.

19

The culmination of modern philosophy is the Hegelian philosophy. The historical necessity and justification of modern philosophy attaches itself, therefore, mainly to the critique of Hegel.

20

The new philosophy has, according to its historical origin, the same task and position toward modern philosophy that the latter had toward theology. The new philosophy is the realization of the Hegelian philosophy or, generally, of the philosophy that prevailed until now, a realization, however, which is at the same time the negation, and indeed the negation without contradiction, of this philosophy.

21

The contradiction of modern philosophy, especially of pantheism, is due to the fact that it is the negation of theology from the viewpoint of theology or the negation of theology that itself is again theology; this contradiction characterizes especially the Hegelian philosophy.

The immaterial being as a pure object of the mind, as a pure entity of the mind, is for modern philosophy and also for Hegelian philosophy the only true and absolute being, that is, God. Even matter, which Spinoza made into an attribute of the divine substance, is a metaphysical object, a pure entity of the mind, for the essential determination of matter as distinguished from the mind, from the activity of thinking—namely, the determination making it a passive being—is taken away here. But Hegel differs from earlier philosophy in that he determines differently the relationship between material, sensuous beings and immaterial beings. The former philosophers and theologians thought of the true, divine being as a being that in itself, by nature, is detached and liberated from sensation and matter. They placed the effort and labor of abstraction and of self-liberation from the sensuous only in themselves, in order to reach that which in itself is already free from the sensuous. To this freedom, they attributed the divine bliss and, to this self-liberation, the virtue of the human being. Hegel, on the other hand, transforms this subjective activity into the self-activity of the divine being. God himself must undertake this labor and, like the heroes of paganism, fight through virtue for his divinity. Only in this way does the liberation of the absolute from matter—which otherwise is only an assumption and a conception—become actuality and truth. But this self-liberation from matter can be attributed to God only if at the same time matter is attributed to him. But how can matter be attributed to God? Only in that he himself attributes it. But in God there is only God. Then, only in that he posits himself as matter, as non-God, that is, as his otherness. Thus, matter is not a preceding opposite of the ego and of spirit, in a way which would be inconceivable; it is the self-alienation of spirit. Thus, matter itself receives spirit and mind; it is taken up into the absolute being as a moment in its life, growth, and development. However, at the same time, matter is nevertheless posited again as an invalid and untrue being in that only the being that restores itself out of this alienation, that is, that detaches itself from sensation and from matter expresses itself as the completed being in its true structure and form. The natural, material, and sensuous—and, indeed, the sensuous, not in the moral and ordinary sense, but in the metaphysical—are to be negated here, as nature which is poisoned by original sin is negated in theology. It is indeed assimilated into reason, the ego, and the spirit; but it is the irrational element in reason, the nonego in the ego—the negative in them. For example, in Schelling, nature in God is the nondivine in God which being in him is apart from him, and, for example, in Cartesian philosophy, the body, although connected with me, that is, with the spirit, is nevertheless apart from me, not belonging to me, that is, to my essence; it is, therefore, irrelevant whether it is connected with me. Matter continues to contradict the being that philosophy presupposes as the true being.

Matter is indeed posited in God, that is, it is posited as God, and to posit matter as God amounts to saying "There is no God," or, what amounts to the same, it is to renounce theology and to recognize the truth of materialism. But at the same time the truth of the essence of theology is nevertheless presupposed. Atheism, the negation of theology, is therefore negated again; that is, theology is restored through philosophy. God is God only because he overcomes and negates matter, that is, the negation of God. And, according to Hegel, only the negation of the negation is the true affirmation. In the end, we are again at the point from which we started—in the bosom of Christian theology. Thus, we already have in the main principle of Hegel's philosophy the principle and outcome of his philosophy of religion, namely, that philosophy does not negate the dogmas of theology, but only restores and mediates them through the negation of rationalism. The secret of the Hegelian dialectic lies, in the last analysis, only in the fact that it negates theology by philosophy and then, in turn, negates philosophy by theology. Theology constitutes the beginning and the end; philosophy stands in the middle as the negation of the first affirmation, but the negation of the negation is theology. At first everything is overthrown, but then everything is put again in its former place; it is the same as with Descartes. The Hegelian philosophy is the last magnificent attempt to restore Christianity, which was lost and wrecked, through philosophy and, indeed, to restore Christianity—as is generally done in the modern era—by identifying it with the negation of Christianity. The much-praised speculative identity of mind and matter, of the infinite and the finite, and of the divine and the human is nothing more than the unfortunate contradiction of the modern era. It is the identity of faith and disbelief, theology and philosophy, religion and atheism, Christianity and paganism, placed on its highest summit, on the summit of metaphysics. This contradiction is placed out of sight and obscured in Hegel only because the negation of God, that is, atheism, is made into an objective determination of God; God is determined as a process, and atheism is determined as a moment in this process. But, by the same token that a faith that is restored from disbelief is hardly a true faith—because it is always a faith attached to its contradiction—so is the God who is restored from his own negation hardly a true God; he is rather a self-contradictory, atheistic God.

22

Just as the divine essence is nothing other than the essence of man liberated from the limits of nature, so is the essence of absolute idealism nothing other than the essence of subjective idealism liberated from the limits, and, indeed, rational limits, of subjectivity, that is, from sensation or objectivity in general. The Hegelian philosophy can therefore be directly derived from Kantian and Fichtean idealism.

Kant says:

When we consider—as, indeed, we ought to—the objects of the senses as mere appearances, so we admit at the same time, by doing so, that they are based on a thing in itself, although we may not know how it is constituted in itself, but only its appearance, that is, the way in which our senses are affected by this unknown something. Thus the understanding, just because it accepts appearances, admits also the existence of things in themselves, and thus we can say that the conception of such beings—which lie at the basis of appearances and are, consequently, mere objects of the mind—is not only possible, but unavoidable.

The objects of the senses, of experience, are thus for the mind mere appearance and not the truth; they do not satisfy the mind, that is, they do not correspond to its essence. The mind is consequently in no way limited in its essence by the senses; otherwise, it would not take the sensuous objects for appearances, but for the straight truth. That which does not satisfy me does not restrict and limit me either. And still the entities of the mind should not be real objects for the mind! Kant's philosophy is the contradiction of subject and object, essence and existence, thought and being. Essence lies here in the mind, whereas existence lies in the senses. Existence without essence is mere appearance—these are the sensuous objects; essence without existence is mere idea—these are the entities of the mind, the noumena. They are thought, but they lack objectivity and existence, at least existence for us. They are the things in themselves, the true things, but they are not real things, and consequently they are also not objects for the mind, that is, they cannot be determined and known by the mind. But what a contradiction to separate the truth from reality and reality from the truth! If we negate this contradiction, we have the philosophy of identity, where the objects of the mind and the things that are thought exist as the true and also as the real things, where the essence and constitution of the objects of the mind correspond to the essence and constitution of the mind or of the subject, and where the subject is no longer limited and conditioned by a substance existing apart from it and contradicting its essence. But the subject, which has no longer an object apart from itself and consequently is no longer limited, is no longer a "finite" subject—no longer the "I" opposite whom an object stands; it is the absolute being whose theological or popular expression is the word "God." It is indeed the same subject and the same "I" as in subjective idealism, but without limits—the "I" that does not seem any longer to be an "I," that is, a subjective being, and therefore is also no longer called "I."

23

Hegelian philosophy is reversed idealism; it is theological idealism, just as the Spinozist philosophy is theological materialism. It placed the essence of the ego apart from the ego, separated from the ego, and objectified as substance, as God. But, by doing that, it expressed again indirectly and reversely the divinity of the "I," making it—as Spinoza made matter—into an attribute or form of the divine substance; man's consciousness of God is the self-consciousness of God. That means that the essence belongs to God and the knowing belongs to man. But in Hegel the essence of God is actually nothing other than the essence of thought, or thought abstracted from the ego, that is, from the one who thinks. Hegelian philosophy made thought—namely, the subjective being conceived, however, without subject, that is, conceived as a being distinct from the subject—into a divine and absolute being.

The secret of "absolute" philosophy is thus the secret of theology. Just as theology transforms the determinations of man into divine determinations—through depriving them of their own determination by which they are what they are—so also in precisely the same way does absolute philosophy transform them.

The thinking of reason can be expected of everybody; in order to think it as absolute—namely, in order to reach the viewpoint that I require—we must abstract from thinking. For him who abstracts, reason immediately ceases to be something subjective, as it is conceived by most people; indeed, it itself can no longer be thought of as something objective, for to be something objective or thought of is possible only in contrast to something that is thinking, from which we here completely abstract; thus, reason becomes through this abstraction the true "in-itself," which indeed stands at the point of indifference of the subjective and the objective.

Thus spoke Schelling, and it is the same with Hegel. The essence of Hegelian logic is thought deprived of its determinateness in which it thinks, i.e., in which lies the activity of subjectivity. The third part of the *Logic* is, and is indeed explicitly called, the subjective logic; and yet the forms of subjectivity that are the object of that part are not to be subjective. The concept, the judgment, the conclusion—indeed, even such particular forms of conclusion and judgment as the problematic or assertoric judgment—are not our concepts, judgments, and conclusions; no, they are objective, absolute forms existing in and for themselves. So does absolute philosophy externalize and alienate from man his own essence and activity! Hence the violence and torture that it inflicts on our minds. We ought not to think of that which is ours as our own; we ought to abstract from the determination by which something is what it is, namely, we ought to think of it without sense and take it in the non-sense of the absolute. Nonsense is the highest essence of theology—of ordinary as well as of speculative theology.

What Hegel disapprovingly observes regarding Fichte's philosophy—namely, that everyone believes the ego to be in himself, that everyone is reminded of himself and yet does not find the ego in himself—is valid for speculative philosophy in general. It comprehends almost all things in a sense by which they are no longer recognized. And the cause of this evil is indeed theology. The divine and absolute being must distinguish itself from finite, that is, real, beings. But we have no determinations for the absolute except the determinations of real things, be they natural or human things. How do these determinations become determinations of the absolute? Only in that they are taken in a sense that differs from their real meaning, that is, in an entirely reversed sense. Everything that exists in finiteness exists also in the absolute; but it exists differently in the absolute. Totally different laws are valid there; that which is for us pure nonsense is reason and wisdom there. Speculation uses the name of a thing without accepting the notion that is linked with it; hence, the boundless arbitrariness of speculation. Speculation excuses its arbitrariness by saying that it chooses for its notions names from the language, to which, however, "ordinary consciousness" attaches concepts that have only a far-fetched similarity to these notions; so now it is the fault of the language. But the fault lies in the matter, in the principle of speculation itself. The contradiction in speculation between name and object, conception and notion, is nothing other than the old theological contradiction between the determinations of the divine being, taken only in a symbolical or analogical sense, and the determinations of the human being, taken in an essential and real sense. At any rate, philosophy need not care about the conceptions that common usage or misuse attaches to a name; philosophy, however, has to bind itself to the determined nature of things, whose signs are names.

24

The identity of thought and being that is the central point of the philosophy of identity is nothing other than the necessary consequence and elaboration of the notion of God as the being whose notion or essence contains existence. Speculative philosophy has only generalized and made into an attribute of thought or of the notion in general what theology made into an exclusive attribute of the notion of God. The identity of thought and being is therefore only the expression of the divinity of reason—that thought or reason is the absolute being, the total of all truth and reality, that there is nothing in contrast to reason, rather that reason is everything just as God is, in strict theology, everything, that is, all essential and true being. But a being that is not distinguished from thought and that is only a predicate or a determination of reason is only an ideated and abstracted being; but in truth it is not being. The identity of thought and being expresses, therefore, only the identity of thought with itself; that means that absolute thought never extricates itself from itself to become being. Being remains in another world. Absolute philosophy has indeed transformed for us the other world of theology into this world, but in turn it has transformed for us this side of the real world into the other world.

The thought of speculative or absolute philosophy—in distinction from itself as the activity of mediation—determines being as immediate and unmediated. For thought—at least for that thought that we have here before us—being is nothing more than this. Thought places being in opposition to itself, but within itself, and thus it invalidates directly and without difficulty the opposition of being vis-à-vis itself; for being, as the opposition of thought within thought, is nothing other than an idea itself. If being is nothing more than being unmediated, if nonmediation alone constitutes its distinction from thought, how easy it is, then, to prove that the determination of nonmediation, namely, being, belongs also to thought! If a mere determination of ideas constitutes the essence of being, how should being be distinguished from thought?

25

The proof that something is has no other meaning than that something is not only thought of. This proof cannot, however, be derived from thought itself. If being is to be added to an object of thought, so must something distinct from thought be added to thought itself.

The example of the difference between a hundred dollars in conception and a hundred dollars in reality—which was chosen by Kant in the critique of the ontological proof to designate the difference between thought and being and which was, however, mocked by Hegel—is essentially quite true. For I have the hundred dollars only in the mind, but the other dollars I have in the hand. The former exist just for me; the latter, however, exist also for others—they can be felt and seen. But only that exists that is at the same time for me and others, on which I and others agree—what is not only mine but is general.

In thought as such, I find myself being in identity with myself; here I am absolute master, and nothing contradicts me; here I am judge and litigant at the same time; here there is consequently no critical difference between the object and my ideas of it. But, if it simply concerns the being of an object, then I cannot consult myself only, but must take the evidence of witnesses who are apart from me. These witnesses that are distinguished from me as thought are the senses. Being is something in which not only I but also others, above all also the object itself, participate. Being means being a subject, being for itself. And it is truly not the same whether I am a subject or only an object, whether I am a being for myself or only a being for another being, that is, only an idea. Where I am a mere object of conception, where I consequently am no longer myself, where I am like a man after death, there I must put up with everything; there it is possible for another person to portray me in a way that would be a true caricature without my being able to protest against it. But, when I am still really existing, then I can thwart him, then I can make him feel and prove to him that there is a vast difference between me as I am in his conception and me as I am in reality, namely, between me as his object and me as a subject. In thought, I am an absolute subject; I accept everything only as my object or predicate, that is, as object or predicate of a thinking self; I am intolerant. In the activity of the senses, on the other hand, I am liberal; I let the object be what I myself am—a subject, a real and self-actualizing being. Only sense and perception give me something as subject.

26

A being that only thinks, and thinks abstractly, has no conception at all of being, of existence, or of reality. Being is the boundary of thought; being as being is not an object of philosophy, at least not of abstract and absolute philosophy. Speculative philosophy itself expresses this indirectly in that for it being is equal to nonbeing—nothing is. Nothing, however, is not an object of thought.

Being as the object of speculative thought is simply the unmediated, that is, the undetermined, object; thus, there is nothing to think about or distinguish in being. But speculative thought is for itself the measure of all reality; it declares only this, in which it finds activity for itself and which provides it with substance for thought, to be something. For abstract thought, being is therefore nothing in itself and for itself, because it is the nothingness of thought, that is, it is nothing for thought—it is the thoughtless. Precisely because of this, this being is also—as it is drawn by speculative philosophy into its domain and claimed as its notion—a pure ghost, standing in absolute contradiction to real being and to that which man understands by being. Namely, by being man understands an existence according to objects and reason, which is being-for-itself, reality, existence, actuality, and objectivity. All these determinations or names express one and the same thing, only from different points of view. Being in thought, without objectivity, reality, or being-for-itself is, of course, nothing; but in this nothingness I only announce the nothingness of my abstraction.

27

"Being" in the Hegelian logic is the "being" of the old metaphysics that is attributed without differentiation to all objects because, according to the old metaphysics, all things agree in that they are. This uniform being is, however, an abstract idea without reality. Being is as varied as the objects that exist.

It is maintained, for example, in a metaphysical theory of Wolf's school, that God, the world, man, the table, the book, and so forth agree with one another in that they are. And Christian Thomasius says: "Being is everywhere the same. Essence is as manifold as the objects." This being that is everywhere the same, without difference and without content, is also the being of the Hegelian logic. Hegel himself observes that the polemic against the identity of being and nothingness derives only from the fact that being is given a definite content. But the consciousness of being is indeed always and necessarily bound to a definite content. If I abstract from the content of being and indeed from every content, since everything is the content of being, then I am left, to be sure, with nothing more than the idea of nothingness. And when, therefore, Hegel reproaches common consciousness for having substituted for being as an object of logic something that does not belong to being, so can he be much more readily reproached for having substituted a groundless abstraction for what man's consciousness rightly and rationally understands as being. Being is not a general notion that can be separated from objects. It is one with that which exists. It is thinkable only through mediation; it is thinkable only through the predicates on which the essence of an object is based. Being is the positing of essence. That which is my essence is my being. The fish exists in water; you cannot, however, separate its essence from this being. Language already identifies being and essence. Only in human life, however, indeed only in abnormal and unfortunate cases, is being separated from essence; only here does it happen that a person's essence is not where his being is. But also precisely because of this separation a person is not truly with his soul where he is really with his body. You are there only where your heart is. All beings, except in cases contrary to nature, like to be where and what they are; that is, their essence is not separated from their being, and their being is not separated from their essence. And consequently you cannot posit being as simply identical with itself in distinction from the variety of essence. Being after its removal from all the essential qualities of the objects is only your conception of being—a being that is made up and invented, without the essence of being.

28

The Hegelian philosophy did not overcome the contradiction of thought and being. That being with which the *Phe-*

nomenology starts stands in the most direct contradiction to real being no less than that being with which the *Logic* starts.

This contradiction becomes apparent in the *Phenomenology* in the form of the *Dies* ["this"] and the *Allgemeinen* ["the general"]; for the particular belongs to being, and the general belongs to thought. In the *Phenomenology,* however, the former and the latter flow together, indistinguishable for thought; but what an immense difference there is between the "this" as an object of abstract thought and the "this" as an object of reality! This wife, for example, is my wife, and this house is my house, although everyone speaks, as I do, of his house and his wife as "this house" and "this wife." The indifference and uniformity of the logical "this" is here interrupted and destroyed by the legal meaning of the word. Were we to accept the logical "this" in natural law, we would directly arrive at a community of goods and wives where there is no difference between this and that and where everyone possesses every woman; we would arrive at the negation of all rights, for rights are founded only on the reality of the difference between this and that.

We have before us in the beginning of the *Phenomenology* nothing other than the contradiction between the word, which is general, and the object, which is always a particular. And the idea that relies only on the word will not overcome this contradiction. Just as the word is not the object, so is the being that is spoken or ideated not real being. Were one to reply that Hegel deals with being, not from the practical viewpoint, as here, but from the theoretical viewpoint, I would be obliged to reciprocate by saying that the practical viewpoint is here completely justified. The question of being is indeed a practical question in which our being participates; it is a question of life and death. And, when we hold fast to our being in the law, so also we do not want logic to take it away from us. It must be recognized by logic also, unless it wants to persevere in its contradiction with real being. By the way, the practical viewpoint—the viewpoint of eating and drinking—is itself taken by the *Phenomenology* in order to refute the truth of sensuous, that is, particular being. But here, also, I owe my existence never to the linguistic or logical bread—bread in itself —but always only to *this* bread, to the "unutterable! " Being that is founded on many such unutterable things is therefore itself something unutterable. It is indeed the ineffable. Where words cease, life first begins, and the secret of being is first disclosed. If, therefore, being unutterable is being irrational, then the whole of existence is irrational because it is always and forever only *this* existence. But it is not irrational. Existence has meaning and rationality for itself, also without being utterable.

29

Thought that "overleaps its otherness"—the "otherness of thought" is, however, being—is thought that oversteps its natural boundaries. Thought overleaps its opposite; this means that thought claims for itself what belongs not to itself but to being. Particularity and individuality, however, belong to being, whereas generality belongs to thought. Thought thus claims for itself particularity; it makes the negation of generality (namely, particularity that is the essential form of sensation) into a moment in thought. So does "abstract" thought or the abstract notion, which has being apart from itself, become a "concrete" notion.

But how does man arrive at this point where thought trespasses into the domain of being? He reaches this point through theology. In God, being is directly bound to the essence or the notion, the form of existence with the generality of the particular. The "concrete notion" is God transformed into the notion. But how does man reach "concrete" or absolute thought from "abstract" thought? How does he arrive at theology from philosophy? The answer to this question was already given by history itself in the transition from ancient pagan philosophy to the so-called neo-Platonic philosophy, for neo-Platonic philosophy differentiates itself from ancient philosophy only in that it is theology, whereas ancient pagan philosophy is only philosophy. Ancient philosophy had reason, the "idea," for its principle; but "the idea was not posited by Plato and Aristotle as the all-comprehending." Ancient philosophy left something existing apart from thought; it left a residue that was not absorbed in thought. The image of this being apart from thought is matter—the substratum of reality. Reason found its boundary in matter. Ancient philosophy still lived in the distinction between thought and being; thought, the mind or the idea, was for it still not the all-comprehending, that is, the unique, exclusive, and absolute reality. The ancient philosophers were still wise men, that is, physiologists, politicians, zoologists; in short, they were anthropologists, not theologians, or at least only partly theologians. To be sure, precisely for this reason they were also at first only partially anthropologists, hence limited and defective anthropologists. To the neo-Platonic philosophers, on the other hand, matter—namely, the material and real world in general—is no longer an authority and a reality. Fatherland, family, worldly ties, and goods in general, which the ancient peripatetic philosophy still counted as man's bliss—all these are nothing for the neo-Platonic sage. He even considers death better than corporeal life; he does not include the body in his essence; he transfers bliss to the soul only and separates himself from all corporeal, in short, external things. When, however, man has nothing else apart from himself, he searches and finds everything in himself; he posits in place of the real world the imaginary and intelligible world in which there is everything that is in the real world, but abstracted and imagined. Even matter can be found in the immaterial world of the neo-Platonists, but it is here only ideated and imagined matter. And, where man has no longer a being apart from himself, he posits a being in his thought, which, though it is a being of thought, still has the properties of a real being, which as an unsensuous being is at the same time a sensuous being and which as a theoretical object is at the same time a practical object. This being is God—the highest good of the neo-Platonists. Man satisfies himself only in essence. He therefore substitutes for himself an ideal being in place of the real being, that is, he now attributes to his conceptions and ideas the essence of the reality that he had relinquished or lost. The imagination is no longer an imagination for him, but the object itself; the image is no longer an image, but the thing itself; thought and idea—reality. Precisely because he no longer relates himself as a subject to a real world as his object, his conceptions become for him objects, beings, spirits, and gods. The more abstract he is, the more negative he is toward the real and the sensuous and the more sensuous he is precisely in abstraction. God, the One—who is the highest object and being of abstraction, thus abstracted from all manifold and differences, that is, sensation—is known by contact and direct presence (Παρουσία). Indeed, as the lowest thing, matter, so also the highest thing, the One, is known through nonknowledge and ignorance. That means that the merely ideated, abstracted, nonsensuous, and supersensuous being is at the same time a really existing, sensuous being.

Just as when a man commits suicide he negates the body, this rational limit of subjectivity, so when he lapses into fantastic and transcendental practice he associates himself with embodied divine and ghostly appearances, namely, he negates in practice the difference between imagination and perception. Thus also is lost theoretically the difference between thought and being, subjective and objective, sensuous and nonsensuous, where matter is for him not a reality and consequently is not a boundary of thinking reason and where for him reason, that is, the intellectual being and the being of subjectivity in general, is in its limitlessness the sole and absolute being. Thought negates everything, but only in order to posit everything in itself. It has no longer a boundary in something apart from itself; therefore, it itself steps out of its immanent and natural boundary. So does reason, the idea, become concrete; namely, that which perception should give is appropriated by thought, and that which is the function and concern of the senses, of perception and of life, becomes the function and concern of thought. So is the concrete made into a predicate of thought and being into a mere determination of thought; for the proposition "the notion is concrete" is identical with the proposition "being is a determination of thought." That which is imagination and fantasy with the neo-Platonists was merely rationalized and transformed by Hegel into concepts. Hegel is not "the German or Christian Aristotle"; he is the German Proclus. Absolute philosophy is the reborn Alexandrian philosophy. According to Hegel's explicit determination, it is not the Aristotelian nor generally ancient pagan philosophy that is the absolute philosophy. It is Alexandrian philosophy that is the Christian philosophy (although to be sure still mixed with pagan ingredients) and the absolute philosophy (although still at the elementary stage of abstracting from concrete self-consciousness).

Let it be further noted that neo-Platonic theology shows with particular clarity that, as the object is, so is the subject, and vice versa; consequently, the object of theology is nothing other than the objectified essence of the subject, that is, of man. For the neo-Platonist, God in the highest degree is the simple, the singular, the simply undetermined and indistinct. He is not a being, but rather above being, for being is still determined by the fact that it is a being. He is not a notion or mind, but rather without and above mind, for mind, too, is determined by the fact that it is mind; and, where there is mind, there also is distinction and separation into thinking and being thought, which consequently cannot occur in the plainly simple. But what is objectively the highest being for the neo-Platonist is also the highest being subjectively; that which he posits in the object, in God, as being he posits in himself as activity and striving. To have no longer any distinction, to have no mind or self, is and means being God. But that which God is the neo-Platonist strives to become; the goal of his activity is to cease "being a self, mind, and reason." Ecstasy or rapture is for the neo-Platonist the highest psychological state of man. This state objectified as being is the divine being. Thus, God is derived only from man, but not conversely, at least originally, man from God. This is shown with particular clarity also in the neo-Platonists' determination of God as the self-sufficient and blissful being, for where else than in the pains and needs of man does this being who is without pain and without needs have its ground and origin? With the lack of need and pain, the imagination and feeling of bliss also collapse. Only in contrast to misery is bliss a reality. Only in man's wretchedness does God have his birthplace. Only from man does God derive all his determinations. God is what man would like to be; he is man's own essence and goal conceived as a real being. Here also lies the distinctiveness of the neo-Platonist as compared to the Stoic, Epicurean, and Skeptic. Absence of passion, bliss, self-sufficiency, freedom, and independence were also the goals of these philosophers, but only as virtues of man; that means that their ground was still the concrete and real man as truth; freedom and bliss should belong to this subject as predicates. Although for the neo-Platonists, too, pagan virtue was still truth—hence the distinction from Christian theology that transferred the bliss, perfection, and the divine likeness of man to the other world—this predicate becomes a subject; that is, an adjective of man becomes a substantive, a real being. Precisely in this manner, real man became also a mere abstraction without flesh and blood, an allegorical figure of the divine being. Plotinus, at least according to the report of his biographer, was ashamed to have a body.

30

The statement that only the "concrete" notion that carries the nature of the real in itself is the true notion expresses the recognition of the truth of concreteness or reality. But because simultaneously the notion—that is, the essence of thought—is presupposed from the start as the absolute and only true being, the real or actual can be recognized only in an indirect way and only as the essential and necessary adjective of the notion. Hegel is a realist, but a purely idealistic realist or, rather, an abstract realist; he is a realist in the abstraction from all reality. He negates thought, namely, abstract thought; but the negation is itself within abstract thought so that the negation of abstraction is itself an abstraction. According to Hegel, philosophy has for an object only "that which is"; but this "is" is itself only an abstracted and ideated "is." Hegel is a thinker who surpasses himself in thought; he wants to grasp the thing itself, but in the thought of the thing. He wants to be apart from thought, but within thought itself —hence the difficulty in comprehending the "concrete" notion.

31

The recognition of the light of reality in the darkness of abstraction is a contradiction; it is the affirmation of the real in its negation. The new philosophy is the philosophy that thinks of the concrete not in an abstract, but in a concrete manner. It is the philosophy that recognizes the real in its reality as true, namely, in a manner corresponding to the essence of the real, and raises it into the principle and object of philosophy. The new philosophy is, therefore, the truth of the Hegelian philosophy and of modern philosophy in general.

The following is a more precise deduction of the historical necessity or genesis of the new philosophy from the old philosophy. According to Hegel, the concrete notion, the idea, is at first only abstract and only in the element of thought; it is the rationalized God of theology before the creation of the world. But, as God manifests, reveals, temporalizes, and actualizes himself, so does the idea realize itself; Hegel is the history of theology transformed into a logical process. Once we arrive, however, with the realization of the idea in the realm of realism, and the truth of the idea is that it is real and that it exists, then we have indeed in existence the criterion of truth: only that which is real is true. And now questions present themselves. What is real? That which is only thought of? That which is only an object of thought and mind. But in this way we will not extricate ourselves from the idea *in abstracto*. An object of thought is also the Platonic idea; an inner object is also the heavenly other world that is an object of faith and imagination. If the reality of thought is ideated reality, then the reality of thought is itself only an idea, and we remain forever in the identity of thought with itself, in idealism. It is an idealism that differentiates itself from subjective idealism only in that it embraces the total content of reality, making it a determinateness of thought. If there is, therefore, real seriousness about the reality of thought or the idea, then something other than itself must be added to it or, the idea as a realized idea must be other than unrealized, as a mere idea; it must be an object, not only for thinking, but also for not-thinking. The self-realization of the idea means that it negates itself and ceases to be a mere idea. What is then this not-thinking, that which is differentiated from thinking? It is the sensuous. The self-realization of the idea means, accordingly, that it makes itself into an object of the senses. The reality of the idea is thus sensation. But reality is the truth of the idea; thus, sensation is the truth of the idea. Precisely so we managed to make sensation a predicate and the idea or thought a subject. But why, then, does the idea represent itself in sensation? Why is it not true when it is not real, that is, sensuous? Is not its truth made, therefore, dependent on sensation? Is not meaning and worth granted to the sensuous for itself, disregarding the fact that it is the reality of the idea? If sensation for itself is nothing, of what need is it to the idea? If only the idea gives value and content to sensation, then sensation is a pure luxury and a trifle; it is only an illusion that the idea presents to itself. But it is not so. The idea is required to realize itself and represent itself in sensation only because, unknowing to the idea, reality and sensation, independent of the idea, are presupposed as the truth. The idea proves its worth through sensation; how would this be possible if sensation were not unconsciously accepted as the truth? Because, however, one starts consciously with the truth of the idea, the truth of sensation is expressed only afterward, and sensation is made only into an attribute of the idea. This is, however, a contradiction, for it is only an attribute and still it gives truth to the idea; namely, it is simultaneously the main thing and an accessory, essence and accident. We save ourselves from this contradiction only if we make the real, that is, the sensuous, into its own subject and give it an absolutely independent, divine, and primary meaning which is not first derived from the idea.

32

The real in its reality or taken as real is the real as an object of the senses; it is the sensuous. Truth, reality, and sensation are identical. Only a sensuous being is a true and real being. Only through the senses, and not through thought for itself, is an object given in a true sense. The object that is given in thought or that is identical with thought is only idea.

Namely, a real object is given to me only where a being that affects me is given to me and where my self-activity—when I start from the viewpoint of thought—finds its boundary or resistance in the activity of another being. The notion of the object is originally nothing other than the notion of another "I"; thus, man in his childhood comprehends all things as freely active and arbitrary beings; therefore, the notion of the object is generally mediated by the notion of the "thou," of the objectified "I." An object, that is, another "I," is given—to speak in Fichtean language—not to the "I," but to the "not-I" in me; for only where I am transformed from an "I" into a "thou," where I am passive, does the conception of an activity existing apart from me, that is, objectivity, arise. But only through the senses is an "I" a "not-I."

The following question is characteristic for the abstract philosophy of earlier times: How can different and independent beings, that is, substances, affect one another? For example, how can the body affect the soul, that is, the "I"? This question was, however, insoluble for them because it was abstracted from sensation and because the substances, which were to affect one another, were abstract beings, pure entities of the mind. The secret of the reciprocal effect is solved only by sensation. Only sensuous beings affect one another. I am an "I" for myself and simultaneously a "thou" for others. This I am, however, only as a sensuous being. The abstract mind, nevertheless, isolates this being-for-itself as substance, atom, "I," or God. It can, therefore, only arbitrarily connect the being-for-others with the being-for-itself; for the necessity of this connection is only sensation, from which, however, the mind abstracts. That of which I think without sensation I think of without and apart from all connection. How can I, therefore, think at the same time of the unconnected as connected?

33

The new philosophy regards and considers being as it is for us, not only as thinking but as really existing beings; thus, it regards being as an object of being, as an object of itself. Being as an object of being—and only this being is being and deserves the name of being—is the being of the senses, perception, feeling, and love. Being is thus a secret of perception, of feeling, and of love.

Only in feeling and in love does "this"—as in "this person" or "this object," that is, the particular—have absolute value and is the finite the infinite; in this alone, and only in this, is the infinite depth, divinity, and truth of love constituted. Only in love is God—who counts the hair on one's head—truth and reality. The Christian God is himself only an abstraction of human love and an image of it. But, precisely because "this" has absolute value only in love, the secret of being discloses itself only in it and not in abstract thought. Love is passion, and only passion is the hallmark of existence. Only that exists which is an object—be it real or possible—of passion. Abstract thought that is without feeling and without passion cancels the difference between being and nonbeing, but this difference—which for thought is an evanescent difference—is a reality for love. Love means nothing other than becoming aware of this difference. To him who loves nothing

—let the object be whatever one wishes—it is all the same whether something does or does not exist. But, by the same token, as being in distinction from nonbeing is given to me only through love and feeling generally, so also is an object in distinction from me given to me only through love. Pain is a loud protest against the identification of the subjective with the objective. The pain of love means that that which is in the imagination is not in reality. The subjective is here the objective, and the imagination is the object; but this ought not to be. This is a contradiction, a falsehood, and a misfortune; hence the longing for the restoration of the true relationship, where the subjective and objective are not identical. Even physical pain expresses this difference evidently enough. The pain of hunger is due only to the fact that there is no object in the stomach; thus the stomach is, as it were, an object to itself, and the empty walls rub against one another instead of against some other substance. Hence, human feelings have no empirical or anthropological significance in the sense of the old transcendent philosophy; they have ontological and metaphysical significance. In feelings—indeed, in the feelings of daily occurrence—the deepest and highest truths are concealed. Thus, love is the true ontological proof of the existence of an object apart from our mind; there is no other proof of being but love and feeling in general. That object whose being affords you pleasure and whose nonbeing affords you pain—that alone exists. The distinction between object and subject, between being and nonbeing, is a distinction just as pleasing as it is painful.

34

The new philosophy rests on the truth of love and feeling. In love and in feeling generally, every man confesses the truth of the new philosophy. The new philosophy itself is basically nothing other than the essence of feeling elevated to consciousness; it only affirms in reason and with reason what every man—the real man—professes in his heart. It is the heart made into mind. The heart does not want abstract, metaphysical, or theological objects; it wants real and sensuous objects and beings.

35

Whereas the old philosophy said, "that which is not thought of does not exist," so does the new philosophy, on the other hand, say, "that which is not loved and cannot be loved does not exist." That, however, which cannot be loved also cannot be worshiped. Only that which can be an object of religion is an object of philosophy.

Love is objectively as well as subjectively the criterion of being, of truth, and of reality. Where there is no love, there is also no truth. And only he who loves something is something; to be nothing and to love nothing are identical. The more one is, the more one loves, and vice versa.

36

Whereas the old philosophy started by saying, "I am an abstract and merely a thinking being to whose essence the body does not belong," the new philosophy, on the other hand, begins by saying, "I am a real, sensuous being and, indeed, the body in its totality is my ego, my essence itself." The old philosopher was thinking, therefore, in continuous contradiction and quarrel with the senses in order to repel the sensuous conceptions from soiling the abstract notions; the new philosopher, on the other hand, thinks in harmony and peace with the senses. The old philosophy confessed the truth of sensation even in the notion of God who comprehends being in himself; for this being was, indeed, supposed to be at the same time a being distinct from being thought, a being apart from mind and thought, a real, objective, that is, sensuous being; it was confessed only in a manner that was hidden, conceptual, unconscious, and reluctant, solely because it was coerced. The new philosophy, on the other hand, recognizes the truth of sensation with joy and consciousness; it is the open-hearted and sensuous philosophy.

37

Modern philosophy searched for something immediately certain. It rejected, therefore, the thinking of the scholastics which was groundless and unfounded and founded philosophy on self-consciousness; that is, it set the thinking being, the ego, and the self-conscious mind in the place of the merely ideated being, in place of God, who is the highest and last being of all scholastic philosophy; for thought is infinitely closer, more present, and certain to the thinking person than is the thought-of. The existence of God is doubtful, and so is generally that which I think; but that I exist, that is, I who think and doubt, is certain. But the self-consciousness of modern philosophy is itself in turn only a being ideated and mediated through abstraction and thus a doubtful being. Certain and immediately assured is only that which is an object of the senses, perception, and feeling.

38

The true and divine is only that that needs no proof, that is certain directly in itself, that directly speaks for itself and convinces in itself, and in which the affirmation that it exists is directly implied; it is that that is plainly decided upon, that is certain and clear as daylight. But only the sensuous is clear as daylight; all doubt and dispute cease only where sensation begins. The secret of immediate knowledge is sensation.

All is mediated, says the Hegelian philosophy. Something is true, however, only when it is no longer mediated, but immediate. Historical epochs arise, therefore, only where that which before was only ideated and mediated becomes an object of immediate and sensuous certainty, namely, that which before was only idea becomes truth. It is scholasticism to make mediation into a divine necessity and an essential attribute of truth. Its necessity is merely a conditional necessity; it is necessary only where a false presupposition still forms the basis, where a truth or a doctrine presents itself in contradiction to a doctrine that is also still taken as true and is respected. The self-mediated truth is the truth that is still attached to its opposite statement. One starts with the opposite statement which, however, is afterward sublated. If, however, the opposite statement is one that is to be sublated and negated, why should I begin with it and not immediately with its negation? Let us take an example. God as God is an abstracted being; he particularizes, determines, and realizes himself in the world and in man; thus, he is concrete and thus, at first, is the abstract being negated. But why should I not then start immediately with the concrete? Why should not that which is certain and proven valid through itself be higher than that which is certain through the negation of its contrary? Who can elevate mediation to necessity and to a law of truth? Only he who himself is still imprisoned by that which is to be negated, who still struggles and quarrels with himself, and who still has not completely made up his mind; in short, only he in whom truth is only talent, a matter of special, even outstanding, ability but not genius and a matter of the whole man. Genius is immediate, sensuous knowledge. What talent has only in the head genius has in the flesh and blood; namely, that which for talent is still an object of thought is for genius an object of the senses.

39

The old absolute philosophy banished the senses to the realm of appearance and finiteness; and yet, in contradiction to this, it determined the absolute, the divine, as the object of art. But the object of art is—mediated in literature and immediate in the visual arts—an object of seeing, hearing, and feeling. Thus, not only the finite and appearing but also the true and divine being is an object of the senses; namely, sense is an organ of the absolute. Art "depicts the truth in sensation"; this means, when rightly comprehended and expressed, that art depicts the truth of sensation.

40

Just as in art, so it is in religion. Sensuous perception, and not the imagination, is the essence of the Christian religion; it is the form and organ of the highest and divine being. Where, however, sensuous perception is taken as the organ of the divine and true being, there the divine being is expressed and recognized as the sensuous being and the sensuous, as the divine being; for, as the subject is, so is the object.

"And the word became flesh and dwelt among us, and we saw its glory." Only for later generations is the object of the Christian religion an object of the imagination and of fantasy; but the original view is restored again. In Heaven, Christ, that is, God, is an object of immediate and sensuous perception; there he is transformed from an object of the imagination and of thought, hence from a spiritual being which he is for us here, into a sensuous, perceptible, and visible being. And this perception is the beginning as well as the end, thus the essence, of Christianity. Speculative philosophy has, therefore, grasped and presented art and religion not in the true light, in the light of reality, but rather only in the twilight of reflection, in that it dissolved sensation—in pursuance of its principle, which is abstraction from sensation—into a mere form-determination of art and religion; art is God in the form-determination of sensuous perception, and religion is God in the form-determination of the imagination. In truth, however, only that which appears to reflection as the form is the essence. Where God appears in the fire and is worshiped, there, in truth, the fire is worshiped as God. God in the fire is nothing other than the essence of fire which, because of its effects and attributes, astounds man; God in man is nothing other than the essence of man. Just so, that which art depicts in the form of sensation is nothing other than the very essence of sensation that is inseparable from this form.

41

Not only "external" things are objects of the senses. Man is given to himself only through the senses; he is an object of himself only as an object of the senses. The identity of subject and object, which in self-consciousness is only an abstract idea, is truth and reality only in man's sensuous perception of man.

We feel not only stones and lumber, flesh and bones; we also feel feelings, in that we press the hands or lips of a feeling being; we hear through our ears not only the rustle of water and the whisper of leaves, but also the soulful voice of love and wisdom; we see not only mirror surfaces and colored spectres, but we also catch a man's glance. Thus, not only the external but also the internal, not only flesh but also mind, not only the object but also the ego are objects of the senses. Everything is, therefore, sensuously perceptible, and although not always immediately so, yet it is perceived through mediation. Although it is not always perceptible through the vulgar and crude senses or through the eyes of the anatomists or chemists, yet it is perceptible through the refined senses or through the eyes of the philosophers. Thus, empiricism rightly derives the origin of our ideas from the senses; only it forgets that the most important and essential sense object of man is man himself; it forgets that only in man's glimpse into man is the light of consciousness and understanding kindled. Idealism is, therefore, in the right when it looks for the origin of the ideas in man; but it is in the wrong when it wants to derive them from the isolated man determined as soul and as a being existing for itself, in short, when it wants to derive them from the "I" without a given sensuous "thou." Only through communication and conversation between man and man do the ideas arise. Not alone, but only with others, does one reach notions and reason in general. Two human beings are needed for the generation of man—of the spiritual as well as of the physical man; the community of man with man is the first principle and criterion of truth and generality. The certainty of the existence of other things apart from me is mediated for me through the certainty of the existence of another human being apart from me. That which I alone perceive I doubt; only that which the other also perceives is certain.

42

The differences between essence and appearance, ground and consequence, substance and accident, necessity and chance, speculative and empirical, do not constitute two realms or worlds of which one is a supersensuous world to which essence belongs and the other is a sensuous world to which appearance belongs; rather, these distinctions all fall within the realm of sensation itself.

Let us take an example from the natural sciences. In the Linnaean botanical system, the first classes are determined by the number of filaments. But already in the eleventh class where twelve to twenty stamens appear—and even more in the class of twenty stamens and of polystamens—the numerical determination becomes irrelevant; it is no longer enumerated. Here we have, therefore, before our eyes in one and the same realm the difference between determined and undetermined, between necessary and irrelevant, rational and irrational plurality. Thus, we need not go beyond sensation in order to reach the boundary of the merely sensuous and empirical in the sense of absolute philosophy; indeed, we must not separate the mind from the senses in order to find the supersensuous, that is, mind and reason, in the sensuous.

43

The sensuous is not, in the sense of speculative philosophy, the immediate; namely, it is not the profane, obvious, and thoughtless that is understood by itself. Immediate, sensuous perception comes much later than the imagination and the fantasy. The first perception of man is merely the perception of the imagination and of the fantasy. The task of philosophy and of science in general consists, therefore, not in leading away from sensuous, that is, real, objects, but rather in leading toward them, not in transforming objects into ideas and conceptions, but rather in making visible, that is, in objectifying, objects that are invisible to ordinary eyes.

Men first see the objects only as they appear to them and not as they are; they do not see themselves in the objects, but only their imaginations of the objects; they posit their own essence in them and do not differentiate the object from the conception of it. The imagination lies closer to the uneducated and subjective man than does intuition, for in intuition he is torn away from himself, whereas in the imagination he remains within himself. But as it is with the imagination, so it is with thought. Men will sooner, and for a much longer time, occupy themselves with heavenly and divine matters than with earthly and human things; that is, sooner and for much longer will they occupy themselves with things translated into ideas than with things in the original and primary language. Only now, in the modern era, has mankind arrived again—as once in Greece after the demise of the Oriental dream world—at the sensuous, that is, the unfalsified and objective perception of the sensuous, that is, of the real; precisely with this, however, it also came to itself; for a man who devotes himself only to entities of the imagination or of abstract thought is himself only an abstract or fantastic, but not a real and true human being. The reality of man depends only on the reality of his object. If you have nothing, you are nothing.

44

Space and time are not mere forms of appearance; they are conditions of being, forms of reason, and laws of existence as well as of thought.

To-be-here is the primary being, the primary determination. Here I am—this is the first sign of a real, living being. The index finger is the signpost from nothingness to being. Here is the first boundary and separation. Here am I, and you are there; we are apart from each other; hence, we can both exist without encroaching on the other; there is room enough. The sun is not where Mercury is, and Mercury is not where Venus is; the eye is not where the ear is; and so on. Where there is no space, there is also no room for any system. The determination of place is the first determination of reason on which every subsequent determination can rest. With the division into different places—and, with space, different places are immediately posited—organized nature begins. Reason orients itself only in space. "Where am I?" is the question of awakening consciousness and the first question of "the wisdom of life." Limitation in space and time is the first virtue, and difference in place is the first difference between that which is decent and that which is indecent. It is the first difference that we teach children, that is, undeveloped human beings, for whom the place is irrelevant, doing everything at every place without difference; so, too, does the fool. Fools, therefore, reach reason when they bind themselves again to a place and a time. To place different things in different places or to distinguish spatially what is qualitatively different is the condition for every economy, even for the spiritual economy. Not to put in the text what belongs in the footnote, not to put at the beginning what belongs at the end, in short, spatial separation and limitation belong also to the wisdom of the writer.

At any rate, we deal here always with a determined place; indeed, nothing more than the determination of a place is here taken into consideration. I cannot separate the place from space if I want to grasp space in its reality. With the question "Where?" the conception of space first arises for me. "Where?" is general and is valid without distinction for every place, and yet "where" is determined. With this "where," the other "where" is simultaneously posited; hence, with the determination of place, the generality of space is simultaneously posited.

But, precisely therefore, the general notion of space is a real and concrete notion only in connection with the determination of place. Hegel accords space, like nature generally, only a negative determination. But to-be-here is positive. I am not there because I am here; this not-being-there is thus only a consequence of the positive, expressive being-here. That here is not there, that one is apart from the other, is only a limit of your imagination, but not a limit in itself. It is a being apart that ought to be and that does not oppose but rather corresponds to reason. In Hegel, however, this being apart is a negative determination because it is the being apart of that which ought not to be apart, for the logical notion as the absolute identity with itself is taken as the truth! Space is, precisely therefore, the negation of the idea and of reason; hence, reason can be re-introduced into space only through its negation. But not only is space not the negation of reason, it provides place for reason and the idea; space is the first sphere of reason. Where there is no spatial being apart, there also is no logical being apart. Or vice versa—if we wish, like Hegel, to go from logic to space—where there is no distinction, there also is no space. Differences in thought must be realized as differentiated things—differentiated things, however, separate spatially from one another. Hence only spatial being apart is the truth of logical distinctions. But those things that are apart from one another can only be thought of one after the other. Real thinking is thinking in space and time. The very negation of space and time (duration of time) falls always within space and time. We wish to save space and time only in order to gain them.

45

Things must not be thought of otherwise than as they appear in reality. That which is separated in reality ought also not to be identical in thought. The exemption of thought and the idea—the world of intellect in neo-Platonism—from the laws of reality is the privilege of theological arbitrariness. The laws of reality are also the laws of thought.

46

The immediate unity of opposite determinations is only possible and valid in abstraction. In reality, opposite statements are always connected through an intermediary notion. This intermediary notion is both the object and the subject of the opposite statements.

Therefore, nothing is easier than to show the unity of opposite predicates; one need only abstract from the object or subject of the opposite statements. The boundary between the opposite statements vanishes with the object; they are now without a bottom and without support, and thus they immediately collapse together. If, for example, I regard being only as such and I abstract from every determination that exists, then of course being equals nothingness for me. The difference, the boundary, between being and nothingness is indeed only the determinant. When I omit that which exists, what is still this mere "is"? But what is valid for this antithesis and its identity is also valid for the identity of all the other antitheses of speculative philosophy.

47

The only means by which opposing and contradicting determinations are united in the same being in a way corresponding to reality is time.

This at least is the case with living beings. Only thus, for example in man, does the contradiction appear whereby I am now occupied and dominated by this determination—that is, this feeling or this intention—and now by another opposing determination. Only where one conception or one feeling displaces another, where no decision and no permanent determination is reached, and where the soul finds itself in a continuous alternation of opposing states does the soul find itself in the hellish pains of contradiction. Were I to unify simultaneously the opposing determinations within myself, they would blunt and neutralize one another like the opposing elements of a chemical process that exist simultaneously yet lose their differences in a neutral product. The pain of contradiction consists precisely in that I am and passionately wish to be now that which in the next instant I, just as vigorously, am not and wish not to be, in that affirmation and negation follow each other, each excluding the other and each affecting me in its full determination and sharpness.

48

The real can be presented in thought not by integers but only by fractions. This difference is normal; it rests on the nature of thought whose essence is generality, in distinction from reality, whose essence is individuality. That this difference, however, does not culminate in an outright contradiction between the ideated and the real is only due to the fact that thought does not follow a straight line in identity with itself, but rather interrupts itself through sensuous perception. Only that thought which is determined and rectified by sensuous perception is real and objective thought—the thought of objective truth.

It is most important to recognize that absolute thought, that is, isolated thought that is separated from sensation, will not get beyond formal identity, namely, the identity of thought with itself; for, although thought or the notion is determined as the unity of opposing determinations, yet these determinations themselves are only abstractions and determinations of ideas, and always identities of thought with itself, that is, only multiples of the identity from which, as the absolute truth, one had started. The other, which the idea posits as opposite to itself, is—as one posited by the idea—not truly and really distinct from the idea and apart from it; at most it is discharged only *pro forma,* as appearance in order to show its liberality; for this otherness of the idea is itself again the idea, only not yet in the form of the idea, not yet posited and realized as idea. Thus, thought for itself alone cannot bring about any positive distinction and opposition to itself; but for this very reason it has also no criterion of truth other than that nothing should contradict the idea or thought; thus, it has only a formal and subjective criterion that does not decide whether the ideated truth is also a real truth. The criterion that decides this is solely perception. One ought, indeed, always to listen to the opponent. But it is precisely sensuous perception that is the opponent of thought. Perception takes matters in a broad sense, whereas thought takes them in a narrow sense. Perception leaves matters in their unlimited freedom, whereas thought gives them laws, which, however, are only too often despotic. Perception enlightens the mind, but determines and decides nothing; thought determines but also often narrows the mind. Perception for itself has no principles, whereas thought for itself has no life. The rule is the concern of thought, whereas the exception to the rule is the concern of perception. Hence, just as only perception that is determined by thought is true perception, so conversely only thought that is broadened and opened by perception is true thought corresponding to the essence of reality. Thought that is continuous and identical with itself lets the world, in contradiction with reality, circle around its center; thought, however, that is interrupted by the observation of the disproportion of this movement, hence, by the anomaly of perception, transforms according to truth this circle into an ellipse. The circle is the symbol and the coat of arms of speculative philosophy, of thought which rests on itself; Hegel's philosophy, too, as is well known, is a circle of circles, although with regard to the planets it posits the orbit—but only because it is compelled to by experience—as "the path of a badly uniform movement"; the ellipse, on the other hand, is the symbol and coat of arms of sensuous philosophy, of thought that rests on perception.

49

The determinations that afford real knowledge are always only those that determine the object by the object itself, namely, by its own individual determinations; thus, they are not general determinations, as the logical-metaphysical determinations are, which determine no object because they extend to all objects without distinction.

Hegel, therefore, quite rightly transformed the logical-metaphysical determinations from determinations of objects into independent determinations, that is, into self-determinations of the concept; he transformed them from predicates, which they were in the old metaphysics, into subjects, thus giving to metaphysics or logic the meaning of self-sufficient and divine knowledge. But it is a contradiction when these logical-metaphysical shadows are made, in the concrete sciences precisely as in the old metaphysics, into determinations of real objects; this is, of course, only possible when either the logical-metaphysical determinations are at the same time always connected to concrete determinations derived from the object itself and, therefore, applicable to it, or when the object is reduced to completely abstract determinations by which it is no longer recognizable.

50

The real in its reality and totality, which is the object of the new philosophy, is also the object only of a real and complete being. The new philosophy has, therefore, as its principle of cognition and as its subject, not the ego, the absolute, abstract mind, in short, not reason for itself alone, but the real and whole being of man. Reality, the subject of reason, is only man. Man thinks, not the ego, not reason. Thus, the new philosophy does not rest on the divinity, that is, the truth, of reason for itself alone; it rests on the divinity, that is, the truth, of the whole man. Or, to put it in another way, the new philosophy does indeed rest also on reason, but on that reason whose essence is the human being; namely, it rests not on a beingless, colorless, and nameless reason, but on reason saturated with the blood of man. Hence, whereas the old philosophy declared that only the rational is the true and real, the new philosophy, on the other hand, declares that only the human is the true and real, for only the human is the rational; man is the measure of reason.

51

The unity of thought and being has meaning and truth only when man is comprehended as the ground and subject of this unity. Only a real being recognizes real objects; only where thought is not the subject of itself but a predicate of a real being is the idea not separated from being. The unity of thought and being is, therefore, not formal, so that being would belong to thought in and for itself as a determination; it depends only on the object, the content of thought.

From this result the following categorical imperatives: Desire not to be a philosopher, as distinct from a man; be nothing else than a thinking man. Do not think as a thinker, that is, with a faculty torn from the totality of the real human being and isolated for itself; think as a living and real being, as one exposed to the vivifying and refreshing waves of the world's oceans. Think in existence, in the world as a member of it, not in the vacuum of abstraction as a solitary monad, as an absolute monarch, as an indifferent, superworldly God; then you can be sure that your ideas are unities of being and thought. How should thought as the activity of a real being not grasp real objects and beings? Only when thought is separated from man and is determined for itself alone do awkward, fruitless, and, from this viewpoint, insoluble questions arise. How does thought arrive at being, that is, at the object? For thought determined for itself alone, that is, posited apart from man, is apart from all ties and connections to the world. You elevate yourself to an object only by lowering yourself to be an object for others. You think only because your ideas themselves can be thought, and they are true only when they pass the test of objectivity, that is, when they are acknowledged by another person apart from you for whom they are an object. You see only as you yourself are a visible being, and you feel only as you yourself are a perceptible being. The world stands open only to an open mind, and the openings of the mind are the senses only. But that thought that is isolated for itself, enclosed in itself, without senses, without and apart from man, is absolute subject that cannot be and ought not be an object for others; for this very reason, however, it will also never find—despite all efforts—a transition to the object and to being; its likelihood is as small as that of a head separated from the body finding a transition by which it can get hold of an object, the reason being that the means, that is, the organs, to do so are lacking.

52

The new philosophy is the complete and absolute dissolution, without any contradiction, of theology into anthropology; for it is the dissolution of theology not only in reason—as was the case in the old philosophy—but also in the heart, in short, in the whole and real being of man. In this respect, the new philosophy is only the necessary result of the old philosophy, for that which was once dissolved in the mind must finally dissolve itself also in the life, heart, and blood of man; but it is also at the same time the truth of the old philosophy and, indeed, a new and independent truth, for only the truth that became flesh and blood is the truth. The old philosophy necessarily reverted to theology; that which is sublated only in the mind and in the notion has still an antithesis in the heart. The new philosophy, on the other hand, can never relapse; that which is dead in both body and soul can never return, not even as a ghost.

53

Man distinguishes himself from the animals not only by thinking. His whole being, rather, constitutes his distinction from the animals. To be sure, he who does not think is not a man; not however, because thinking is the cause, but only because it is a necessary consequence and attribute of the human essence.

So we need not also here reach beyond the realm of sensation in order to recognize man as a being ranking above the animals. Man is not a particular being, like the animals, but a universal being; he is not, then, a limited and restricted being, but rather an unlimited and free being, for universality, absoluteness, and freedom are inseparable. This freedom does not lie in a special faculty, that is, will, nor does universality lie in a special faculty of thinking, that is, reason; this freedom and this universality extend themselves over man's total being. The senses of the animal are indeed keener than those of man, but only in respect to certain objects that necessarily relate to the needs of the animal; and they are keener precisely because of this determination, this excluding limitation to a definite object. Man does not have the sense of smell of a hunting dog or of a raven, but only because his sense of smell is a sense embracing all kinds of smell; hence it is a freer sense which, however, is indifferent to particular smells. But, wherever a sense is elevated above the limits of particularity and its bondage to needs, it is elevated to an independent and theoretical significance and dignity; universal sense is understanding; universal sensation, mind. Even the lowest senses, smell and taste, elevate themselves in man to intellectual and scientific acts. The smell and taste of things are objects of natural science. Indeed, even the stomach of man, which we view so contemptuously, is not animal but human because it is a universal being that is not limited to certain kinds of food. Precisely thereby is man free of the frenzy of voracity with which an animal throws itself over its prey. Leave man his head but give him the stomach of a lion or a horse, and he certainly will cease to be a man. A limited stomach conforms only to a limited, that is, animal, sense. The moral and rational relationship of man to the stomach consists therefore of treating the stomach, not as an animal being, but as a human being. He who concludes his view of man with the stomach, placing it in the class of animals, also consigns man, as far as eating is concerned, to bestiality.

54

The new philosophy makes man—with the inclusion of nature as the foundation of man—the unique, universal and highest object of philosophy. It thus makes anthropology, with the inclusion of physiology, the universal science.

55

Art, religion, philosophy, and science are only manifestations or revelations of the true human essence. Man, the complete and true man, is only he who possesses a sense that is esthetic or artistic, religious or moral, philosophic or scientific; in general, only he who excludes from himself nothing essentially human is man. "Homo sum, humani nihil a me alienum puto"—this sentence, taken in its most universal and highest meaning, is the motto of the new philosophy.

56

The absolute philosophy of identity has completely displaced the viewpoint of truth. The natural viewpoint of man, the viewpoint of the distinction between I and thou, subject and object, is the true and absolute viewpoint; consequently, it is also the viewpoint of philosophy.

57

The unity of mind and heart, according to the truth, consists, not in extinguishing or glossing over their difference, but rather only in that the essential object of the heart is also the essential object of the mind; namely, it consists only in the identity of the objects. The new philosophy—which makes the essential and highest object of the heart and of man likewise the most essential and highest object of the mind—thus establishes a rational unity of mind and heart, of thought and life.

58

Truth does not exist in thought for itself or in knowledge for itself. Truth is only the totality of human life and of the human essence.

59

The single man for himself possesses the essence of man neither in himself as a moral being nor in himself as a thinking being. The essence of man is contained only in the community and unity of man with man; it is a unity, however, which rests only on the reality of the distinction between I and thou.

60

Solitude is finiteness and limitation; community is freedom and infinity. Man for himself is man (in the ordinary sense); man with man—the unity of I and thou—is God.

61

The absolute philosopher said, or at least thought, of

himself—of course as a thinker and not as man—*La vérité c'est moi,* in a way similar to the saying, *L'état c'est moi* of the absolute monarch, and the saying, *L'être c'est moi* of the absolute God. The human philosopher, on the other hand, says: even in thinking and in being a philosopher, I am a man among men.

62

The true dialectic is not a monologue of a solitary thinker with himself; it is a dialogue between I and thou.

63

The Trinity was the highest mystery and the focal point of absolute philosophy and religion. But as was historically and philosophically shown with regard to the essence of Christianity, the secret of the Trinity is the secret of communal and social life; it is the secret of the necessity of the "thou" for an "I"; it is the truth that no being—be it man, God, mind, or ego—is for itself alone a true, perfect, and absolute being, that truth and perfection are only the connection and unity of beings equal in their essence. The highest and last principle of philosophy is, therefore, the unity of man with man. All essential relations—the principles of various sciences—are only different kinds and ways of this unity.

64

The old philosophy possesses a double truth—the truth for itself, which was not concerned with man, that is, philosophy, and the truth for man, that is, religion. The new philosophy, on the other hand, as the philosophy of man is also essentially the philosophy for man; it possesses an essentially practical—and indeed in the highest sense practical—tendency without damaging the dignity and independence of theory, indeed in closest harmony with it. It takes the place of religion and has the essence of religion within itself. In truth, it is itself religion.

65

So far, the attempts at philosophical reform have differed more or less from the old philosophy only in form, but not in substance. The indispensable condition of a really new philosophy, that is, an independent philosophy corresponding to the needs of mankind and of the future, is, however, that it will differentiate itself in its essence from the old philosophy.

Index

The Library of Liberal Arts

AESCHYLUS, Prometheus Bound

D'ALEMBERT, J., Preliminary Discourse to the Encyclopedia of Diderot

AQUINAS, ST. T., The Principles of Nature, On Being and Essence, On Free Choice, *and* On the Virtues in General

ARISTOTLE, Nicomachean Ethics
On Poetry and Music
On Poetry and Style

ARNAULD, A., The Art of Thinking (Port-Royal Logic)

AUGUSTINE, ST., On Christian Doctrine
On Free Choice of the Will

BACON, F., The New Organon

BARON and BLAU, eds., Judaism

BAUDELAIRE, C., The Prophetic Muse: Critical Essays of Baudelaire

BAYLE, P., Historical and Critical Dictionary (Selections)

BECCARIA, C., On Crimes and Punishments

BERGSON, H., Duration and Simultaneity
Introduction to Metaphysics

BERKELEY, G., Principles, Dialogues, *and* Philosophical Correspondence
Principles of Human Knowledge
Three Dialogues Between Hylas and Philonous
Works on Vision

BOCCACCIO, G., On Poetry

BOETHIUS, The Consolation of Philosophy

BOILEAU, N., Selected Criticism

BOLINGBROKE, H., The Idea of a Patriot King

BONAVENTURA, ST., The Mind's Road to God

BOSANQUET, B., Three Lectures on Aesthetic

BOWMAN, A., The Absurdity of Christianity

BRADLEY, F., Ethical Studies

BURKE, E., An Appeal from the New to the Old Whigs
Reflections on the Revolution in France
Selected Writings and Speeches on America

BURKE, K., Permanence and Change

BUTLER, J., Five Sermons

CALVIN, J., On the Christian Faith
On God and Political Duty

CATULLUS, Odi et Amo: Complete Poetry

CICERO, On the Commonwealth

Cid, The Epic of the

CROCE, B., Guide to Aesthetics
DESCARTES, R., Discourse on Method
Discourse on Method *and* Meditations
Discourse on Method, Optics, Geometry, *and* Meteorology
Meditations
Philosophical Essays
Rules for the Direction of the Mind
DEWEY, J., On Experience, Nature, and Freedom
DIDEROT, D., Encyclopedia (Selections)
Rameau's Nephew and Other Works
DOSTOEVSKI, F., The Grand Inquisitor
DRYDEN, J., An Essay of Dramatic Poesy and Other Essays
DUNS SCOTUS, J., Philosophical Writings
EPICTETUS, The Enchiridion
EPICURUS, Letters, Principal Doctrines, *and* Vatican Sayings
ERASMUS, D., Ten Colloquies
EURIPIDES, Electra
FEUERBACH, L., Principles of the Philosophy of the Future
FICHTE, J., The Vocation of Man
GOETHE, J., Faust I and II (verse)
Faust I (prose)
Faust II (prose)
GRANT, F., ed., Ancient Roman Religion
Hellenistic Religions
GRIMMELSHAUSEN, J., Simplicius Simplicissimus
GROTIUS, H., Prolegomena to The Law of War and Peace
HAMILTON, C., ed., Buddhism
HANSLICK, E., The Beautiful in Music
HENDEL, C., Jean-Jacques Rousseau: Moralist
Studies in the Philosophy of David Hume
HERDER, J., God, Some Conversations
HESIOD, Theogony
HOBBES, T., Leviathan I and II
HORACE, The Odes of Horace *and* The Centennial Hymn
HUME, D., Dialogues Concerning Natural Religion
Inquiry Concerning Human Understanding
Inquiry Concerning the Principles of Morals
Of the Standard of Taste, and Other Essays
Philosophical Historian
Political Essays
JEFFERY, A., ed., Islam
KANT, I., Analytic of the Beautiful
Critique of Practical Reason
First Introduction to the Critique of Judgment
Foundations of the Metaphysics of Morals
The Metaphysical Elements of Justice, Part I of *Metaphysik der Sitten*
The Metaphysical Principles of Virtue, Part II of *Metaphysik der Sitten*
On History
Perpetual Peace
Prolegomena to Any Future Metaphysics
KLEIST, H., The Prince of Homburg
LAO TZU, The Way of Lao Tzu
Lazarillo de Tormes, The Life of

LEIBNIZ, G., Monadology and Other Philosophical Essays
LESSING, G., Laocoön
LOCKE, J., A Letter Concerning Toleration
Second Treatise of Government
LONGINUS, On Great Writing (On the Sublime)
LUCIAN, Selected Works
LUCRETIUS, On Nature
MACHIAVELLI, N., The Art of War
Mandragola
MARCUS AURELIUS, Meditations
MEAD, G., Selected Writings
MILL, J., An Essay on Government
MILL, J. S., Autobiography
Considerations on Representative Government
Nature *and* Utility of Religion
On Liberty
On the Logic of the Moral Sciences
Theism
Utilitarianism
MOLIÈRE, Tartuffe
MONTESQUIEU, C., The Persian Letters
NIETZSCHE, F., The Use and Abuse of History
NOVALIS, Hymns to the Night and Other Writings
OCKHAM, W., Philosophical Writings
PAINE, T., The Age of Reason
PALEY, W., Natural Theology
PARKINSON, T., ed., Masterworks of Prose
PICO DELLA MIRANDOLA, On the Dignity of Man, On Being and the One, *and* Heptaplus

PLATO, Epistles
Euthydemus
Euthyphro, Apology, Crito
Gorgias
Meno
Phaedo
Phaedrus
Protagoras
Statesman
Symposium
Theaetetus
Timaeus
Commentaries:
BLUCK, R., Plato's Phaedo
CORNFORD, F., Plato and Parmenides
Plato's Cosmology
Plato's Theory of Knowledge
HACKFORTH, R., Plato's Examination of Pleasure
Plato's Phaedo
Plato's Phaedrus
PLAUTUS, The Haunted House
The Menaechmi
The Rope
POPE, A., An Essay on Man
POST, C., ed., Significant Cases in British Constitutional Law
QUINTILIAN, On the Early Education of the Citizen-Orator
REYNOLDS, J., Discourses on Art
Roman Drama, Copley and Hadas, trans.
ROSENMEYER, OSTWALD, and HALPORN, The Meters of Greek and Latin Poetry
RUSSELL, B., Philosophy of Science
Sappho, The Poems of

SCHILLER, J., Wilhelm Tell
SCHLEGEL, J., On Imitation and Other Essays
SCHNEIDER, H., Sources of Contemporary Philosophical Realism in America
SCHOPENHAUER, A., On the Basis of Morality
Freedom of the Will
SELBY-BIGGE, L., British Moralists
SENECA, Medea
Oedipus
Thyestes
SHAFTESBURY, A., Characteristics
SHELLEY, P., A Defence of Poetry
SMITH, A., The Wealth of Nations (Selections)
Song of Roland, Terry, trans.
SOPHOCLES, Electra
SPIEGELBERG, H., The Socratic Enigma
SPINOZA, B., Earlier Philosophical Writings
On the Improvement of the Understanding
TERENCE, The Brothers
The Eunuch
The Mother-in-Law
Phormio
The Self-Tormentor
The Woman of Andros
Three Greek Romances, Hadas, trans.
TOLSTOY, L., What is Art?
VERGIL, Aeneid
VICO, G. B., On the Study Methods Our Time
VOLTAIRE, Philosophical Letters
WHITEHEAD, A., Interpretation of Science
WOLFF, C., Preliminary Discourse on Philosophy in General
XENOPHON, Recollections of Socrates *and* Socrates' Defense Before the Jury